invite
PRESS

EVERYBODY NEEDS SOME CAVE TIME

JORGE ACEVEDO

EVERY BODY NEEDS SOME CAVE TIME

MEETING GOD IN DARK PLACES

invite
PRESS

Plano, Texas

To the people of Grace Church

My last paper in seminary in May of 1988 was a reflection on my impending new role as a pastor in a local church. In June of 1988, I was "assigned" as an ordained pastor on the staff of a large United Methodist Church in Central Florida by my bishop. In that paper, I wrote that the title *Pastor* cannot be demanded but earned. Grace is free, but the title of pastor must be won. I cannot make anyone call me Pastor Jorge even if my name is on the church sign, the church letterhead, and my business card. *Pastor* is an earned title, even to an "assigned" clergyperson.

Over the thirty-nine years of my ministry, I have been privileged to serve at four churches: Trinity Hill United Methodist in Lexington, Kentucky; First United Methodist Church in Kissimmee, Florida; Christ Church in Fort Lauderdale, Florida; and Grace Church in Cape Coral and Fort Myers, Florida. Upon arriving at each church, I saw as one of my first assignments to live into not only my ministry assignment but also the sacred title of pastor. Truth be told, some days I did a lot better than other days, but by the grace of God, in each of these four communities of faith, people allowed me the holy privilege of being their pastor. It is a role and title that I do not hold onto tightly because it is so precious and fragile.

For twenty-seven of those thirty-nine years of ministry, I was privileged to live and love with the amazing people of Grace Church. I came to serve alongside them on September 1, 1996, at the ripe old age of thirty-six, having never served as a lead pastor. Those saints loved me and brought the best out of me. One of my mentors, Bishop Dick Wills, used to say, "Great pastors don't make great churches. Great churches make great pastors." Grace Church made me a better pastor.

I dedicate this book to you, the people of Grace Church. In our long, slow walk together, we have gotten a front row seat to a miracle. God's Spirit hovered over our dry bones, and new life was born. Many lost people were found. Found people were grown in Christ. The lonely were enveloped in Christian community. The poor were welcomed and lifted up. The addicted were delivered and freed. Leaders were raised up and released. Children and youth were transformed. Today, our community looks more like God's dream. God did this through you. So, I want to say, "Thank you." Thank you for the twenty-seven-year journey. But my dear Grace Church family, never forget this common yet, in this case, true saying: "The best is yet to come." Your best days are in front of you. I have loved being your pastor.

Contents

Foreword by
Rev. Matthew Hartsfield

Lead Pastor, Bay Hope Church

During my college years I enjoyed scuba diving. I primarily went diving on the shallow reefs off the coast of Ft. Lauderdale. Occasionally I would get the opportunity to dive in the Florida Keys. Every dive was a beautiful, new adventure.

However, before I could dive, I was required to complete a PADI certification course. We studied all the forms of diving: open water diving, deep water diving, night diving, wall diving, and ice diving, to name a few. Regardless of the type of diving, the number one rule of diving is always to use the buddy system. You never dive alone.

The most fascinating, and potentially most dangerous, form of diving we studied was cave diving. In Florida we have multiple opportunities for this thrilling sport. And even though I've never experienced it myself, I remember to this day (forty years later!) the heightened importance of the buddy system while cave diving. There are entirely different checklists and responsibilities for learning the buddy system when undertaking cave dives. Your life depends on each other. I would never want to dive into a cave without a highly qualified buddy.

Jorge Acevedo is the most qualified buddy I know to successfully navigate the caves of real life. Over the course of thirty-five-plus years we have ventured into multiple caves with each other: pastoral, spiritual, emotional, mental, and relational. I would trust my life with Jorge in these caves that can be just as dangerous as the actual physical caves into which divers plunge.

As a friend, covenant group brother, and pastoral colleague, I have had the privilege of getting to know Jorge up-close and personal. He's the real deal. There's not a single pretentious bone in his body. His authenticity is matched only by his hard-earned wisdom from doing cave time over decades of life.

In this candid and insightful book, Jorge will be your trusted dive buddy. Go ahead, venture into the exploration of these caves of life. You will be blessed by the journey.

Foreword by
Dr. E. Dale Locke

Founding/Lead Pastor, Community of Hope

In 2014, I traveled with my brother-in-law and his two sons for a week-long fly-fishing expedition in off-grid Alaska. It was the trip of a lifetime for anyone, but especially for me. A third generation Floridian, I had never been to Alaska, much less used a float plane to chase down salmon and rainbow trout.

Beyond the chance to deepen my relationship with my Texas relatives and enjoy the incredible fishing and world-class food at the lodge every evening, there were two experiences from the trip that stand out above all the rest. One was a forty-eight-degree plunge with my two nephews into the river the lodge was built near, and the second, a day-long fly-fishing trip on some of the smaller rivers feeding through the Katmai National Forest. Both experiences included a lack of brilliance on my part.

The Katmai National Forest, and especially the Brooks River region, has fish in abundance. But what it also has, perhaps in excess even more than fish, are bears. Lots of bears. And to be clear: This was my first-ever wilderness experience chasing big fish, one in which at least half of my energy was devoted to making sure nothing was chasing me! The old joke about not really needing to outrun the bear, just outrun your buddy, took on new meaning for me that day.

However, the most interesting part of that afternoon was when our fishing guide talked us into leaving the larger river for a little tributary that trailed off into the woods. Here he said was the best fishing we'd find in the forest. Memories of topography of that area, and the pristine condition of what he walked us down into, will stay with me forever. So will the moment when he asked us to stop, carefully walked in front of us, picked up two stones, and began to bang them together as he moved forward. Being the Floridian that I am, I asked our younger guide, "What are you doing?" To which he replied, "Working hard not to surprise any nearby bears. Bears don't like to be surprised." Almost on command, all of us grabbed rocks and pitched in to help our trail guide increase our chances to fish yet another day! The lesson of that day is clear: Don't travel dangerous terrain without a qualified and experienced guide to assist you. And when it comes to the twists, turns, and uncertainties of our lives in these times, I can offer to you no better trail guide than that of my best friend, Pastor Jorge Acevedo.

I've known Jorge for thirty-seven years. We met in seminary both pursuing the call of God on our lives—two Floridians with a similar call and a more similar personality. We became fast friends, really fast. Over the years, I've had a front row seat to see God use this man in profound and incredible ways. Because he's human, I've walked with Jorge through some of the most difficult experiences life can bring our way. And so, whether we're talking about the next leadership challenge in front of you, or the bitter headwinds life brings, I've seen my best friend drop his shoulder into the wind, and many times drop his knee to the ground, and come through the situation with the fresh wisdom God provides to all who seek Him. This is the wisdom Jorge comes now to offer each of us, through these pages.

Need strength for today and bright hope for tomorrow? Keep reading the latest from the pen and the heart of my best friend. You might find just what you need to get through whatever trail you're on.

Acknowledgements

Grace Church began a unique sermon preparation strategy in 2007 shortly after becoming a multisite church. Until then, each pastor had locked him or herself up in the pastoral study and banged out a message for each campus. In 2006, we sensed the Spirit leading us to build a teaching team assigned with the sacred task of preparing a sermon for our campuses. This new team has been developed and refined over the years.

This teaching team did the initial work on a sermon series entitled "Everybody Does Some Cave Time" for the 2016 season of Lent. In room 3 of the Cape Coral campus from 8:30 to 10:30 am, we shared from scripture, commentaries, books, articles, websites, and our life experiences. We noisily wrestled with the text and attempted to make the message clear and practical for God's people who call Grace Church their spiritual home. We laughed and cried, argued and agreed, and together wove a beautiful homiletical tapestry to the glory of God and the good of God's people. In many ways, this book, a reworking of this message series, is the collaborative work of an amazing team of brilliant spiritual leaders, and I want to acknowledge them here. A special thank you to Rev. Wes Olds and Rev. Kevin Griffin, my pastoral colleagues at the Cape Coral campus of Grace Church who were the primary writers with me on this material. Also, thank you to Rev. Arlene Jackson, Rev. Shari Lacey, Rev.

Patti Nemazie, Rev. Mike Winchell, Pastor Taylor Brown, and Tom Kapla for their remarkable input in writing the original material. You all are amazing.

Introduction

A few years ago I was invited to speak at a friend's church in Ohio. Our hosts, Philip and Sarah, took my wife Cheryl and me to Ohio Caverns in West Liberty, Ohio. This beautiful place is known as having "America's Most Colorful Caverns." It was a great adventure to walk the mile-long path into the cave and out the other side. As with most cave tours, there came a time in the adventure when the guide shut off all the lights. It was the darkest place I have ever experienced. You couldn't see a shadow or even your hand right in front of your face. Caves are remarkable places.

As you read the Bible, caves seem to be a place where biblical characters find themselves in some of the most trying as well as most exhilarating circumstances. This book is by design a journey into seven caves. It's a companion for you, a sort of spiritual inventory as you slowly walk to the final cave, the empty garden tomb. So, for the next seven chapters, you are going to look at seven caves in the Bible. Each cave will be connected to a biblical character with a unique story that I believe will connect with your story too.

During this cave exploration adventure, also known as *spelunking*, we will travel to the cave of anger with Samson as well as the cave of fear with David. We will journey to the cave of depression with Elijah, and we will also climb into the cave of temptation with Jesus. We'll enter the cave of grief with Martha and Mary and the cave of hopelessness with Mary Magdalene. And then lastly, we will celebrate with Jesus, but *this* time in the cave of resurrection! It's going to be an awesome pilgrimage.

But remember—walk slowly. We follow a Messiah who changed the world at three miles per hour. We miss so much when we run all the way to Easter's empty cave. As my colleagues in the rooms of recovery say, "The joy is in the journey." Let's walk to and sit in each of these caves for a while. In the dark places, we can find our true spiritual condition. In the still places, we can meet with the God who wants to meet with us.

Let me begin by giving us a definition of caves for our journey. *A cave can be either a hiding place or a holy place.* Let that sink in. A cave can be either a place of concealing or a place of healing. Each of the caves in these Bible stories was a place where someone chose how they would respond in their cave. Would the cave be a place to elude God or a place to encounter God? Would it be a place to hide from God or a place to seek God? Would they run from God, or would they respond to God? Some were hiding, eluding, and living on the run from God, but they forgot the old adage, "Everywhere I go, there I am!" Everywhere we go, God also goes. A psalm writer wrote, "Where can I go from your presence? If I go to heaven, you are there. If I go to hell, you are there" (Psalm 139:7-8). Everywhere we go, every season of life, every dark place can become a place where we seek and meet God and are transformed. The cave can become a place to encounter the God who loves us most and best.

Friends, it doesn't matter whether our cave is a cave of anger, fear, depression, temptation, or hopelessness, God wants to meet us where we are and transform us into the woman or man we can become in Him. But here's the one truth that we need to settle in our minds: *Everybody needs some cave time!* At times throughout your life, you may find yourself in a cave of one form or another. Whether it's a hiding place or a holy place depends on you. Whether you elude

God or encounter God depends on you. Whether you hide from God or seek God during your cave time depends on you. And here's the best news of all. God does some of God's best work in caves.

Chapter 1: With Samson in the Cave of Anger

Those who are hot-tempered stir up strife, but those who are slow to anger calm contention.
—Proverbs 15:18

When things go wrong, anger is there. This is anger. He will make sure the world knows anger is in control. But what you really need to watch out for is when he's out-of-control.[1]
Voiceover narration, teaser video, Disney Pixar's Inside Out

When our youngest son, Nathan, began his adolescence, he took up the "family business" of addiction. I am a first-generation follower of Jesus, but for generations most of the adult males in our family have sadly and tragically abused alcohol, drugs, and sex. God's saving and sanctifying grace rescued and continues to deliver me from these unhealthy compulsive behaviors. Sadly, whether it was by genetics or environment, our sweet Nathan got swept up into the world of drugs as a teen.

His middle and high school years were constant battles between his will and ours. Whether it was related to school, work, or cleaning his room, it seemed that almost everything was a fight. Shortly before

---

1.   *Get to Know Your "Inside Out" Emotions: Anger,* YouTube video, DisneyPixar, 2015, http://www.youtube.com/watch?v=-HQIg3ZwAs0.

turning eighteen, he was arrested at Walmart for stealing. Ironically, he had the money for the items in his pocket. It made no sense. Shortly after he turned eighteen, he was arrested and sent to jail for the first time for having drug paraphernalia in his car. From the ages of eighteen to twenty-one, he experienced a series of arrests and car accidents. Many nights he snuck out of our home to use drugs and party with his friends. Knowing my family history of addictions, we were, of course, deeply concerned. But frankly, we were caught up in our own codependent behavior, which would soon also be challenged.

When my eighty-year-old parents moved in with us, this further changed the dynamics in our home. Sadly, they too got swept up in a codependent relationship with Nathan. Soon, I started noticing that items from our garage were missing. Then, it was jewelry that belonged to my wife, Cheryl. Finally in December of 2009, Cheryl and I discovered that $3500 was missing from our savings account. Our home was a deeply trusting home, and Nathan knew the pin number to our accounts. Nathan's addiction was out of control.

When we discovered that Nathan had stolen money from our account to buy drugs, I was enraged and on the verge of being out of control. I came as close to physically hurting my son Nathan as I had ever come. I'll never forget that night. With my clenched right fist drawn back and my left hand around his throat, I shook with anger and screamed venomous words at him.

Incongruent to this, these events occurred during the same year the Foundation for Evangelism named me "The Distinguished Evangelist of the United Methodist Church." Catch the sad irony? To the world, I was a successful pastor, but behind the closed door of our family home, there was nothing distinguished about my uncontrolled anger that night.

It would take years of therapy, recovery, spiritual direction, and accountability with other Christ-followers for God to heal me and help me recover from this dark place, as well as to heal and recover my relationship with my sweet son, Nathan, who today by the grace of God is sober and has a great relationship with my wife and me.

Anger can be a good thing, at least according to the American Psychological Association.[2] It can help us express negative feelings. But most of us prefer the unhealthy kind. Out of control anger abandons us in a cave of misery, leaving behind a wake of broken relationships and damaged souls. Regrettably, I know of out-of-control anger. I have painful memories of thinking and saying things to my wife, Cheryl, and my sons, Nathan and Daniel, that make me shudder and fill me with sadness. I've had my fair share of heart-wrenching, guilt-producing, shame-enhancing, out-of-control anger moments. This kind of anger is a relational and spiritual killer.

What is the difference between "good anger" and "out-of-control anger"? How do we learn to control our anger?

A Miracle Boy with an Anger Problem

The Bible tells a story of a man with an anger problem. More than a thousand years before Jesus was born, Samson's birth was miraculous too. Like Jesus, Samson was born with a God-initiated mission. Judges 13:2-5 gives us the details:

> There was a certain man of Zorah, of the tribe of the Danites, whose name was Manoah. His wife was barren, having borne no children. And the angel of the Lord appeared to the woman and said to her, "Although you are barren, having borne no children, you shall conceive and bear a son. Now be careful not to drink wine or strong drink, or to eat anything unclean, for you shall conceive and bear a son. No

---

2. "Anger," American Psychological Association, http://www.apa.org/topics/anger#:~:text=Anger%20is%20an%20emotion%20characterized,excessive%20anger%20can%20cause%20problems.

razor is to come on his head, for the boy shall be a Nazirite
to God from birth. It is he who shall begin to deliver Israel
from the hand of the Philistines."

This couple who struggled with infertility was promised a son.
In the ancient Near East, being without a child was a personal and
social tragedy for any woman. The barren wife would experience re-
jection, scorn, and shame from her husband, family, and community. The promise of a son to Manoah and his unnamed wife gave
them not just a bundle of joy but a whole new lease on life.

God placed a condition on the happy couple, though: their miracle baby boy was to be a Nazarite. Centuries before, Moses, speaking on God's behalf in Numbers 6:1-8, had given to God's people
the requirements for being such a set-aside woman or man called
"Nazarite." Beyond being a teetotaler, having unshorn hair, and
staying away from dead bodies, Moses gives this last overarching re-
quirement in verse 8: "All their days as Nazirites they are holy to the
Lord." Nazarites were to be consecrated and set apart for God. But
here's the deal. These requirements for Moses and the Hebrews were
short term. Jews would make a Nazarite vow for a season, perhaps
like the choice you make in Lent to give up chocolate or commit to
seven weeks of fasting. Manoah and his wife had to, at some point
in Samson's life, break the news to him that his vow was for life. I
thought having the sex talk with my sons was hard. Imagine telling
your teenage son that he can never drink, cut his hair (he might like
that one), or hang out at the cemetery. This might somewhat explain
why Samson had an anger issue. Lent is for seven weeks. Samson had
to give up this stuff for his entire lifetime!

Yet, this child had a special giftedness in his life. In the words
of Darth Vader, "The Force is strong with this one."[3] The Spirit of

---

3. *Star Wars: A New Hope* (1977), http://www.starwars.com/
films/star-wars-episode-iv-a-new-hope.

God was given to Samson in a unique way. He was born with strong potential for God and good. Yet, Samson also had other forces and spirits at work within him. Out-of-control rage lurked within the boy wonder, too. He was both sacred and sinful, fabulous and faulty. In this season of their lives as a nation, Israel is being brutalized by the pagan Philistines and needs help. God works out God's divine purpose for Israel through the bumbling and fumbling Samson. Judges 14 begins with Samson making a demand of his parents to marry a certain Philistine woman he had spotted. His is a brattish request, a "I want what I want, and I want it now" moment. In verse 3, his parents point to a holier way: "Is there not a woman among your kin, or among all our people, that you must go to take a wife from the uncircumcised Philistines?"

Centuries earlier, Moses, the great deliverer of God's people and declarer of God's ways, had been crystal clear. As a "set apart" people, Israel was not to intermarry with other nations. To do so would open the door for God's people to follow after foreign gods (Exodus 34:11-16). The stubborn Samson would not have it. "Get her for me, because she pleases me," the brat demanded.

The author of Judges gives us this commentary to assure us that in spite of Samson's brattish disobedient choices, God was working through Samson to carry out a divine mission on behalf of Israel. The author writes in Judges 14:4, "His father and mother did not know that this was from the Lord, for he was seeking a pretext to act against the Philistines. At that time the Philistines had dominion over Israel." This moment has a Romans 8:28 feel to it. "We know that all things work together for good for those who love God, who are called according to his purpose." God's mysterious providence would overrule Samson's sin and weakness to accomplish God's purposes.

In a moment straight out of *Palestine's Got Talent*, Samson and his parents head to the Philistine town where the woman who caught his eye presumably lived, in order to make negotiations and arrangements for the nuptials. On the journey, Samson is separated from his parents when a lion attacks him. Judges 14:6 says: "The Spirit of the Lord rushed on him, and he tore the lion apart barehanded as one might tear apart a kid. But he did not tell his father or his mother what he had done." That's "talent!" It seems obvious and surprising in the text that Samson did not know he had this kind of strength. Old Testament commentator, David Jackman, writes of Samson's might:

> There follows the first demonstration of Samson's supernatural strength and we are intended to be surprised about it, as Samson was by the beast. We find this difficult because we have been reared on centuries of Christian art which has usually delighted to represent Sampson as our Old Testament Rambo or Mr. Universe. In fact, the text would seem to indicate the opposite. Up to this point there has been no indication of Samson's proverbial strength. Indeed, had he spent hours "pumping iron" to build a magnificent physique, Delilah would hardly have needed to ask him, "Please tell me where your great strength lies." (16:6). It was a mystery to everybody. But the text explains it to us. "The Spirit of the Lord came mightily upon him" (v. 6).[4]

In keeping with the superhero theme, this story rings of Spiderman first learning that he can hang from the ceiling. It was unexpected. It was a surprising gift, a grace for the young man with super-human strength from the Spirit. Like you and me, Samson had been given supernatural abilities that were expressed despite his deep flaws.

With this new discovery of strength, Samson and his parents visit with the Philistine young woman, and it appears that a marriage was arranged. As the story progresses, Samson returns sometime later

---

4. David Jackman, *Mastering the Old Testament: Judges/Ruth,* vol. 7 (Dallas: Word, Inc., 1991), 223–24.

to his soon-to-be Philistine bride, and along the way he passes by the rotting carcass of the dead lion he had torn apart earlier. He notices bees and honey in the dead carcass and scoops out some of the honey and eats it. Some might assume that Samson violates his Nazarite vow by touching the dead lion, though technically it forbids touching a dead human. Regardless, Samson comes across as reckless and a bit cavalier. Could some of this kind of impulsive lack of self-control contribute to his out-of-control rage?

Clearly, what happens next sheds light on Samson's shadow side. Samson throws a kind of bachelor party that most Bible translations call a "feast," but more accurately could be described as a "drinking party."[5] His careless choice to drink clearly violates his parent's promise to raise their son as a Nazarite. In a kind of brash drinking game, Samson gives a riddle to his thirty groomsmen with a bet attached to it. If in seven days they can solve his riddle, they will receive thirty undergarments and thirty festive outer garments. If they do not solve the riddle in seven days, they must give Samson the same. "Deal?" asks Samson. "Deal!" say the thirty Philistine men.

Samson gives them the riddle. "Out of the eater came something to eat. Out of the strong came something sweet" (14:14). The answer to the brainteaser was "Lion" and "Honey," clearly pointing to the lion that Samson had torn asunder with his bare hands and the honey that the bees deposited in the carcass. It begs to be asked, What was Samson's motive in choosing this riddle? Did Samson give them this riddle so that he might boast of his supernatural strength? Was arrogance over his Spirit-induced strength settling in on the groom to be? Proverbs 16:18 wisely cautions, *"Pride goes before destruction, and a haughty spirit before a fall."* As selfishness raised its ugly head in Samson's demand for a Philistine bride from his parents, pride is peeking its head up again here.

---

5. Jackman, *Mastering the Old Testament*, 226.

Seven days pass and none of the thirty men can solve the riddle, so they collude together to have Samson's new Philistine bride use her wiles to get the riddle's solution from her new husband. Yet "collude" may be too soft a word in this context. The men actually threaten to kill her and her father if she didn't comply. No doubt traumatized, Samson's wife convinces him to give her the solution on the last day of the contest, day seven. Putting aside her motivation to stay alive for a moment, another of Samson's defects of character is blazingly clear. He could be easily manipulated. Later, another woman named Delilah would put similar pressure on Samson for secrets of even greater consequence to the strong man. So, armed with the answer to the riddle, his wife tells the thirty men, who on the last day of the feast, deceitfully solve the riddle.

Now Samson is on the hook for the thirty pieces of under and outer garments. It was time to pay his debt. The author of Judges tells us how Samson would settle his debt. In Judges 14:19, we read: "Then the Spirit of the Lord rushed on him, and he went down to Ashkelon. He killed thirty men of the town, took their spoil, and gave the festal garments to those who had explained the riddle."Yes, you read that right. Samson is once again endowed with superhuman strength from the Spirit, so he goes to a neighboring village, kills thirty men singlehandedly, takes their under and outer garments, and gives them to the deceitful men of his new bride's village.[6]

Samson's anger is out of control. In Judges 14:19, it simply states that after killing thirty men to pay his gambling debt, "In hot anger he went back to his father's house." The chapter ends with Samson returning home to his mother and father acting as if noth-

---

6. There are obvious theological problems with God's Spirit endowing Samson with strength that he used to kill thirty men. How does Samson's revenge intersect with God's character and purposes? It's hard to reconcile. Some argue that because Samson was an Israelite judge, his actions were justified because it was exacted against the pagan Philistines. I frankly find this unsatisfactory. But is this not the kind of theological messiness that we go through today as well? Reconciling God's will, character, and purposes with human free will and sin is not easy. It's mysterious, and it's almost always hard to wrap our heads around.

ing had happened, but not before one last jab is given to Samson by the Philistines. Verse 20 says, *"And Samson's wife was given to his companion, who had been his best man."* Ouch. Samson will not be a happy camper. More out-of-control rage would be triggered by these circumstances.

Anger Is Contagious

In 2013, when I was on my sabbatical in England, my wife, Cheryl, and I were at the London Zoo. Cheryl was in a shop looking at a few things, and I was sitting underneath a tree near a playground filled with elementary school aged children. I overheard a very frustrated teacher say to a student, "Why are you making me so angry?" It struck me as an absurd declaration! "Why are you making me so angry?" A little child was "making" her, a full-grown, educated adult, angry! A seven-year-old was to blame for the anger of a forty-seven-year-old teacher. But sitting there underneath that tree, I began to reflect on how many times have I said or thought this very same and very absurd question. "Cheryl . . . Daniel . . . Nathan . . . Mom . . . Dad . . . why are you making me so angry?" This is called blame shifting! Samson would reveal this responsibility-avoiding behavior in a future meetup with the Philistines.

In the next chapter of Samson's life, he returns to the city where he had lost his bet to the thirty men in order to reclaim his wife. He seems to act as if nothing had happened. The bride's father had thought Samson hated her, so he gave his daughter in marriage to his best man. This sends Samson over the top in another fit of rage. Now listen to what Samson says in Judges 15:3 after he gets this news. "Samson said to them, 'This time, when I do mischief to the Philistines, I will be without blame.'" In other words, "You made me do this!" Isn't that just like an out-of-control, rage-filled, angry person? He or she plays the oldest game in the book. Samson shifts the blame: "What I'm getting ready to do is your fault!"

We as humans inherited this tendency toward blame shifting from our first parents, Adam and Eve. Do you remember what happened after the whole eating the fruit from the tree in the center of the Garden debacle? Naked and ashamed, they sewed fig leaves together to cover themselves. Genesis 3:8-13 gives us the back and forth dialogue between God and his cherished creatures:

> They heard the sound of the LORD God walking in the garden at the time of the evening breeze, and the man and his wife hid themselves from the presence of the LORD God among the trees of the garden. But the LORD God called to the man and said to him, "Where are you?" He said, "I heard the sound of you in the garden, and I was afraid, because I was naked, and I hid myself." He said, "Who told you that you were naked? Have you eaten from the tree of which I commanded you not to eat?" The man said, "The woman whom you gave to be with me, she gave me fruit from the tree, and I ate." Then the LORD God said to the woman, "What is this that you have done?" The woman said, "The serpent tricked me, and I ate."

The man blames the woman, and the woman blames the serpent. Blame shifting! Similarly, Samson told his ex-wife's dad, "You can't blame me for what I'm about to do. It's your fault!" Blame shifting! It's one of the sad, sick games angry people play.

Here's what Samson's blame shifting led to. His anger consumed him. Listen to what he does in Judges 15:4-5:

> So Samson went and caught three hundred foxes and took some torches; and he turned the foxes tail-to-tail and put a torch between each pair of tails. When he had set fire to the torches, he let the foxes go into the standing grain of

the Philistines, and burned up the shocks and the standing grain, as well as the vineyards and olive groves.

That's quite a trick! Samson's rage literally turns into a fire that burnt down the vineyards and the olive fields of the town. You have to admit, his angry actions were inventive. 150 pairs of foxes with their tails tied together and torches lit between them is some strategy, but it does seem like a bit of an overreach. Yet isn't that what unhealthy and unholy anger does in and through us? There was nothing distinguished about me raising my fist to my child and nothing honorable about Samson's fox-torch response either. This kind of anger scorches relationships and leaves a wake of destruction.

But here's the consequence: the rage does not end with Samson's revenge. It spreads. Judges 15:6, says," Then the Philistines asked, "Who has done this?" And they said, "Samson, the son-in-law of the Timnite, because he has taken Samson's wife and given her to his companion." So the Philistines came up and burned her and her father." It was bad enough that Samson's rage caused a literal fire. What's even worse is that Samson's rage was infectious. It not only consumed him but spilled over into the townspeople who burned with rage against the father and his daughter. "Samson burned us, so we'll burn them," they fumed. The fire of anger consumed Samson and the entire town. Anger is contagious.

One of my gravest concerns for our world today is the amount of anger being inappropriately expressed over all kinds of issues, including politics, race, and human sexuality. It does not matter what side of the aisle you stand on related to these issues. Each party callously lobs anger bombs at one another. Disagreement about principles and policies turn into character defamation. Social media becomes a platform for vitriol. Friends post things about supposed friends on social media platforms that I doubt they would say to their faces. This kind of excessive anger can consume us and others. Anger can become an out-of-control wildfire.

With the embers of the fire still smoldering, Samson says something about the reciprocating nature of out-of-control rage. In Judges 15:7-8a (NLT), we read what Samson says and then does to the angry citizens of the Philistine town of Timnah: "'Because you did this,' Samson vowed, 'I won't rest until I take my revenge on you!'" So, he attacked the Philistines with great fury and killed many of them. This is what I like to call "the hit back tendency." It's our propensity to want to get even. "You hurt me, so I'll hurt you."

Retrace the story with me. Samson arrogantly bets on a seemingly unsolvable riddle that, because of his own character defects, is deceitfully solved. This leads to the senseless genocide of thirty innocent men from a neighboring village to repay his lost wager. When Samson receives the news that his wife has been given to another man in marriage, in rage he lights their citizens' fields on fire. The citizens in turn kill Samson's ex-wife and father, and Samson, in a bloodthirsty fit of retribution, kills many of the Philistines. The unknown author of the famous maxim "An eye-for-eye and tooth-for-tooth leads to a world of the blind and toothless" got it right.

Out-of-control anger leads to vengeance. It is an insane, never-ending cycle.

Trapped in a Cave of Anger

I've met people who were so angry that they burned down all of their relationships with people who loved them until they found themselves utterly isolated. Years ago, I befriended a young man in our church. He was married to a delightful woman, and together they were raising their young daughter. My friend was an amazing person who owned and successfully ran a small business with several employees. On top of that, he was an amazing follower of Jesus who loved to serve.

One big problem haunted my friend's life. Like me, he struggled with an addiction to drugs and alcohol. He would go months without drinking, but not with any kind of recovery program—what we call "white knuckling it." His extended periods of sobriety relied on sheer will power. Sadly, he would come to our big Friday night recovery experience, help serve in the kitchen, stand in the back of the big room listening to the lessons and testimonies on recovery, but never sit in the small groups where the "magic" of recovery happens. It is by being toe-to-toe and knee-to-knee with other brothers who are finding healing from their disease that my friend could have found his deliverance. He was close, but not close enough.

Several times over the years, he would call me in a panic because his wife had said, "Enough," or he had lost a big job because he was drunk. Some crisis would bring him to my doorstep. "Let's go to a meeting" I would suggest. Sometimes he would say "Yes," but most often, it was, "I'll think about it," followed by weeks of no contact. The last time I saw my friend, he was not my friend of old. He was crazed with the ravages of alcoholism and drug abuse. He stood at my front door, screamed obscenities at me, slammed the door, and left. A few months later, I got the call from his best friend that my terrorized friend died alone of an overdose in a warehouse.

I wept that day because I loved my friend. I thought of those brief moments when he was lucid and in his right mind. We would talk about his life. Buried just beneath the surface was rage over the injustices he had experienced as a child and later as an adult. The "demons" that drove my dear friend to drink and to use drugs were the traumatic and unresolved experiences of his life. Drinking and drugging silenced the beast within . . . at least for a while. But ultimately, the beast took his life. My friend died alone, imprisoned in his cave of anger and addiction.

Samson found himself trapped in a cave of anger (Judges 15:8). I envision an angry and exhausted Samson isolating himself following his latest fit of rage. Samson's cave of anger became a cave of isolation. Isolation happens when anger turns venomous. Who wants to be around an angry person anyhow?

A cave became a prison cell for this man born with such great potential for God. The rage festered inside this child of God and person of worth[7] and left him alone. Uncontrolled anger, unbridled rage, and unrestrained bitterness consumed and confined this man born of promise. Interestingly enough, one Bible dictionary translates his cave, *etam*, to mean "lair of wild beasts."[8] Isn't that what unchecked anger made Samson—a wild beast? And, didn't his anger fuel a wildfire that turned the citizens of the Philistine town of Timnah into a "lair of wild beasts?" In the end, Samson found himself confined to his own hellish cave.

Good and Angry?

The learning behind Samson's story isn't "Do I get angry?" but rather "What do I do with my anger?" Or maybe better yet, "What do I let anger do to me and to others?"

Samson's father-in-law gave away his wife to his best man. Samson had a good reason to be mad. That's the tricky thing about anger. Things happen to us that should make us angry. When political bullies flex their strength and invade countries, we should get mad. When sex traffickers kidnap innocent girls and boys and exploit them, we should get mad. When in our family of origin bullies flex their strength and invade our well-being, we should get mad. When emotional traffickers kidnap our innocence, we should get mad.

---

7. This is a phrase that health counselor, Bonnie Crandall, coined to describe the belovedness of all persons.

8. William Smith, ed., *A Dictionary of the Bible* (Hartford, CT: S. S. Scranton & Co., 1898), 257.

When we experience abuse and trauma like my friend did and like Samson did, we should get angry.

Remember, included in *The American Psychological Association* definition for anger is also this statement: "Anger can be a good thing. It can give you a way to express negative feelings, for example, or motivate you to find solutions to problems."[9] Anger helps us name injustice whether it is social or personal. There is a way to be "good and angry."

How do we become "good and mad" and not "bad and mad?" How can we resist Samson's "hit back" propensity? Having disagreements with people about difficult circumstances does not have to break out into hand-to-hand combat. In Ephesians 4:26b, Paul helps us when he writes, "Be angry but do not sin." For the apprentice of Jesus, anger and holiness can be held in the same body. But how? Look at what Paul writes earlier in Ephesians 4:21-24 (NLT). This will really help us as we seek to live free from out-of-control anger.

> Since you have heard about Jesus and have learned the truth that comes from him, throw off your old sinful nature and your former way of life, which is corrupted by lust and deception. Instead, let the Spirit renew your thoughts and attitudes. Put on your new nature, created to be like God— truly righteous and holy.

Paul uses the image of clothing to describe our lives. He teaches us to "take off" our old ratty, sinful, devilish clothes and to "put on" our new clothes that were given to us by Jesus. Notice the second line: "Instead, let the Spirit renew your thoughts and attitudes." The Holy Spirit can renew our old angry thoughts and attitudes. The Bible teaches that the same Spirit that raised Jesus' lifeless body from the dead lives inside of Christ-followers (Romans 8:11). We have a

---

9. "Anger," American Psychological Association, http://www.apa.org/topics/anger#:~:text=Anger%20is%20an%20emotion%20characterized,excessive%20anger%20can%20cause%20problems.

power inside of us so that we don't have to live by the mantra, "Why are you making me so mad?" With the Holy Spirit living inside of us, we do not have to be controlled by anger.

After declaring that we can be angry and not sin, Paul offers a practical insight: "And, do not let the sun go down on your anger and do not make room for the devil" (Eph 4:26-27.) He teaches us to practice what one of my professors called "the 24-hour rule." This practice helps us deal with the anger-provoking situations in our life "in real time." Practically, it means navigating anger as quickly as possible to keep it from growing roots into our soul and derailing our lives later. Isn't it true that unresolved anger gives evil "room" in our lives?

Right after Easter a few years ago, I told a colleague at the church I serve who has been one of my dearest and longest friends something insignificant regarding our Easter planning and services, and he responded with a short, cutting word. I let it go, but the more I sat in it, the more hurt I became. A week later, during our weekly coaching time, I told my friend about it. My dear friend wept and sought forgiveness. Now, I could have kept it "inside" and not made the first move, but the devil, the world, and my flesh would have co-operated together to make me miserable and give me a "heart at war" toward my colleague instead of a "heart at peace."[10] This is living by the mantra, "Keep my side of the street clean."

Initiating a conversation, no matter how uncomfortable, is key. Not letting too much time pass was essential to the health of our relationship. Don't let unresolved anger give the devil a foothold in your life. When my anger gets out of control, I am a pawn in Satan's hand. It destroys my relationships and steals my joy. But anger dealt with, in the power of the Holy Spirit, does not allow the devil to take hold of me.

---

10. This is the language from the classic book on resolving conflict, *The Anatomy of Peace* (San Francisco, CA: Berrett-Koehler Publishers, Inc., 2008).

In Ephesians 4:25-32, Paul writes,

> Let no evil talk come out of your mouths but only what is useful for building up, as there is need, so that your words may give grace to those who hear. And do not grieve the Holy Spirit of God, with which you were marked with a seal for the day of redemption. Put away from you all bitterness and wrath and anger and wrangling and slander, together with all malice. Be kind to one another, tenderhearted, forgiving one another, as God in Christ has forgiven you.

In the second line Paul writes, "And do not grieve the Holy Spirit of God." The Greek word translated "grieve" means "to pain" or "to sorrow." Paul is saying that with our anger, we can bring pain and sorrow to the Holy Spirit, the third person of the mysterious Trinity. R. T. Kendall writes, "Grieving the Spirit refers to actions of ours that hinder the Spirit from being Himself—from being what he could be in us."[11]

So, how do we grieve the Holy Spirit? Notice what Paul writes about in the verses surrounding this:

- Don't let evil words come out of our mouths.
- Use words that build up and give grace.
- Get rid of bitterness, wrath, anger, wrangling and slander. These are mostly done with words.
- Instead be kind, tenderhearted, and forgiving, which are mostly communicated with words.

Paul is saying that we grieve the Holy Spirit when we use our words inappropriately with others and thus, the Holy Spirit cannot be who the Holy Spirit might be within us.

---

11. R. T. Kendall, *The Sensitivity of the Spirit* (Lake Mary, FL: Charisma House, 2002), 27.

Several months ago, my father-in-law, John, had a stroke and was in a long-term care facility. One evening, the care facility made a mistake that sent our family into a panic for several hours. John needed hospital care. The facility appropriately sent him by ambulance to get medical treatment. That was not the blunder. The blunder was that they lost him. I mean, they really lost him. It seems the ambulance driver took him to a brand new, stand-alone emergency facility outside of the normal health care system in our county, and the care facility did not track it. When we called, they sadly and simply said, "We don't know where he is." We were besides ourselves with concern. It was late at night, so my wife and I dressed and drove to the hospital where he would normally have been taken. After some inquiries, we discovered that he had been taken to a stand-alone facility.

After seeing him and making sure he was OK, I got mad. I had "anger fantasies" of what I was going to say to the administration of the long-term care facility, but by the grace of God, I had time not only to calm down but to pray. And do you know what Jesus had the audacity to tell me? He told me to be filled with love. How dare he? I wanted "a pound of flesh." The next morning, my son and I went to the meeting with hearts at peace and not hearts at war. I was able to name the injustice, and the facility administration owned their mistakes. We were able to extend grace. The Spirit of God was not grieved, because I resisted evil, bitter, wrathful, angry, wrangling, and slanderous words. Instead, in the power of the Holy Spirit, I used words that built up and extended grace. They were words that were kind, tenderhearted, and forgiving. I had emerged from the cave of anger.

Many of us know of Francis, born in the Italian village of Assisi in 1182, famously known as St. Francis of Assisi. What you may not know is that he grew up in a wealthy, luxurious family. One day he met a beggar, and God used this encounter to change Francis' life.

Heartbroken at the beggar's plight, he became a follower of Jesus. He entered the ministry without the blessing of his family and friends. For two years, Francis literally lived in a cave. In this cave, he studied the Bible and prayed. It was from this cave haven that Francis fell in love with God's creation, especially animals. This was a cave of peace and serenity.

After emerging from this cave, Francis spent his life in service to others. His famous prayer, the "Prayer of St. Francis," creates space in the hearts of potentially angry women and men to "be angry yet not sin." It transforms a cave of anger into a meeting place with the Prince of Peace who makes it a cave of serenity in the soul of Jesus followers, in which they can deal with their anger, pain, and grief. Make this your prayer.

> Lord, make me an instrument of your peace;
> where there is hatred, let me sow love;
> when there is injury, pardon;
> where there is doubt, faith;
> where there is despair, hope;
> where there is darkness, light;
> and where there is sadness, joy.
> Grant that I may not so much seek to be consoled as to console;
> to be understood, as to understand,
> to be loved as to love;
> for it is in giving that we receive,
> it is in pardoning that we are pardoned,
> and it is in dying that we are born to eternal life.

Chapter 2: With David in the Cave of Fear

For God has not given us a spirit of fear and timidity,
but of power, love, and self-discipline.
—2 Timothy 1:7 (NLT)

We turn our attention now to one of the most common and crippling of all caves: the cave of fear. Now, life is full of fears and a quick search online reveals that we as human beings suffer from thousands (yes, thousands) of phobias. Certain circumstances and situations can paralyze us with phobic fear. On the long list of phobias, I saw arachnophobia, or the fear of spiders, and aviophobia, or fear of flying. Have you ever heard of "ailurophobia?" It's the fear of cats. I've got this one. Cats are really spooky to me. I think when cats are looking at you, they are thinking, "How could I kill this person?" We human beings tend to fear lots of things. The cave of fear beckons to all of us to enter it and it wants to kill us too.

I've come to believe through my own personal experience and my ministry as a pastor that fear has become the dominating reality in our culture. We are afraid of climate change and political change. We are afraid of transferable viruses and computer viruses. Gas prices as well as the price of healthy relationships leave us paralyzed in fear. And just because you are a follower of Jesus, this does not exempt you from fear. In spite of the fact that 365 times (one for every day of the year), the Bible tells followers of God, "Fear not," we often live fearful lives. Fear is an equal opportunity offender. Everybody gets afraid.

Now, let me be clear about something. Fear is not necessarily a bad thing. Fear can motivate us to protect ourselves during times of real and imminent danger. Say for example, you hear a gun shot. Your brain in milliseconds tells your body to increase your heart rate, start sweating, and take off running! It's called the "fight or flight reaction." This reaction can often keep us alive. We need to pay attention to our fears for they may be a gift.

But sadly, there are some of us who have crippling, unhealthy, and often uncontrollable fears. It's like our "fight or flight reaction" is stuck in the "on" position all of the time. Some of us are imprisoned by our fears, and we need the help of medication, counselors, and therapists who can help us find healing when our fears became debilitating and overwhelming. You are not a bad or weak person if this is you. Something is wrong, and it can be fixed. By the grace of God, we can be healed of our debilitating fears.

But here's what we know to be true. All of us need a remedy for what we might call the "ordinary" fears that assault our everyday serenity. So, we are going to look at a person in the Bible named David who understood fear. He entered the cave of fear and it became a place of encounter with God. We first meet him when Israel's current King, Saul, becomes disobedient. The prophet Samuel tells Saul that he and his family will lose his throne. The prophet is then sent by God to Bethlehem on a recruiting mission to anoint one of the sons of a man named Jesse to replace the wayward king. We pick up Samuel's headhunting adventure in 1 Samuel 16.

When Samuel the prophet arrives at Jesse's home, the father brings seven of his sons to appear before Samuel. The first born, Eliab, was apparently a fine physical specimen, and God whispered this cautionary word to the prophet, "Do not look on his appearance or on the height of his stature, because I have rejected him; for the Lord does not see as mortals see; they look on the outward appearance, but the Lord looks on the heart." (1 Samuel 16:7). One by one the other six boys pass in front of the man of God, but none of them are the chosen one whom God had directed Samuel to find. Samuel then asks Jesse an odd question. "Are these all the sons you have?" Jesse's response to Samuel is telling. "There remains yet the youngest, but he is keeping the sheep" (1 Samuel 16:11). The word for "youngest" in Hebrew comes from the root word *qaton* and carries with it the idea of being insignificant. It's like dear old dad said, "Well, there is the inconsequential one out back watching the sheep" (notice not "my son David"). So, in one fell swoop, David is unnumbered and unnamed by his father. Talk about having "daddy issues." This alone would ding your self-worth and become a platform for fears.

I love the commentary in 1 Samuel 16:12-13. Samuel sent for David. Now he was ruddy, and had beautiful eyes, and was handsome. The Lord said, "Rise and anoint him; for this is the one." Then Samuel took the horn of oil and anointed him in the presence of his brothers; and the Spirit of the Lord came mightily upon David from that day forward.

Ruddy with beautiful eyes and handsome! Right there in front of his neglectful father and seven astonished older brothers, David is anointed by Samuel. It's not clear whether David and his family knew that Samuel was anointing him to be the next King, but Samuel did. And remember, the wayward King Saul is still on the throne!

Soon after this, the armies of the unruly King Saul are locked in a battle with their bitter enemies, the Philistines, and the battle comes to a standstill. For forty days, a giant Philistine warrior named Goliath came out to taunt the Israelite army and mock God. One day, the previously forgotten and now-anointed David is delivering food to his brothers on the front lines and he overhears the giant mocking the army of Israel. He sees the soldiers afraid and volunteers to fight him. In an Ultimate Fighting Championship showdown for the ages, David kills Goliath with his slingshot. He cuts off Goliath's head with his own sword, and the Philistines tuck tail and run away.

This event accomplished two things. It made David a celebrity, and it made King Saul jealous. Crowds began to sing songs about David. The lyrics to this most downloaded tune went like this: "Saul has killed his thousands, and David his ten thousands" (1 Samuel 18:7). Ouch! This went over really well with Saul, right? Soon, a jealous and rage-filled Saul begins to plot David's death, and David has to go on the run and hide in fear.

We pick up the story in 1 Samuel 21:10-13 as David flees to enemy Philistine territory:

> David rose and fled that day from Saul; he went to King Achish of Gath. The servants of Achish said to him, "Is this not David the king of the land? Did they not sing to one another of him in dances, 'Saul has killed his thousands, and David his ten thousands'?" David took these words to heart and was very much afraid of King Achish of Gath. So he changed his behavior before them; he pretended to be mad when in their presence. He scratched marks on the doors of the gate, and let his spittle run down his beard.

What a scene. David is so afraid that he returns to the land and people of Goliath. How bad does it have to be at home for it to seem better to live with your arch nemesis? And once there, David has to pretend to be a madman, so that they won't kill him. King Achish upon seeing David as a madman says to his servants, "Look, you see the man is mad; why then have you brought him to me? Do I lack madmen, that you have brought this fellow to play the madman in my presence? Shall this fellow come into my house?" (1 Samuel 21:14-15). In other words, "I've got enough crazy people in my life.

I don't need one more." With this David leaves Gath. This is when David enters his cave of fear.

We know that fear is crippling. Like an anchor, it weighs us down and keeps us spiritually, emotionally, and relationally stunted. I've discovered in my own life that fear is like the white noise of my soul. It's bothersome but I get used to it. As I write this, I am in a transition. For twenty-seven years, I have been the lead pastor of Grace Church and soon I will transition into a new ministry of coaching, consulting, writing, and speaking. All I've ever wanted to be is a pastor, and it's all I've ever known as an adult. The volume of the white noise of fear slowly increases in my being as the day of transition draws closer. Financial and relational insecurities raise their ugly head inside of me. You see, fear wants to put a stranglehold on my soul. And this is not good for me and for those whom I love. Undiagnosed fear steals my belovedness in Christ, destroys my self-awareness, and damages my relationships with others.

The Power of Remembering

After David's Academy Award–winning role as a mad man in Gath, while still on the run from a real mad man, King Saul, 1 Samuel 22:1a tells us the location to which David relocated. *David left there and escaped to the cave of Adullam.* Let me tell you about the cave of Adullam. It is a rocky cave in the wilderness that overlooks the valley of Elah. Now get this, the valley of Elah was the exact spot where David had defeated Goliath years before. While David was in his cave of fear, right in front of David was *the* place where he had singlehandedly in the name of God defeated the greatest warrior on the planet.

Can you imagine David looking over that valley and remembering the day that God gave him victory? That was the day David stood eyeball-to-belly-button with Goliath and boldly declared:

You come to me with sword and spear and javelin; but I
come to you in the name of the Lord of hosts, the God of
the armies of Israel, whom you have defied. This very day
the Lord will deliver you into my hand, and I will strike you
down and cut off your head; and I will give the dead bodies
of the Philistine army this very day to the birds of the air and
to the wild animals of the earth, so that all the earth may
know that there is a God in Israel, and that all this assembly
may know that the Lord does not save by sword and spear;
for the battle is the Lord's and he will give you into our hand
(1 Samuel 17:45-47).

When wave after wave of paralyzing fear in his present circumstances overwhelmed the unnamed and unnumbered son of Jesse,
David would look out and look back to remember God's past victories. It's the spiritual impulse the Bible gives us over and over again—
to remember. It's why the Church was instructed by Jesus during the
Lord's Supper to "do this in remembrance of me" (Luke 22:19).

One of the gifts of being the pastor at the same church for
twenty-seven years is that I have the gift of perspective. I didn't have
it in 1996 however when I came to be their pastor. My first day
at Grace Church, we had no vision, a few hundred people, owed
1.2 million dollars, and had $29.16 in the checking account! Things
were bad. But our ever-faithful God got us through back then! That
first week, I invited the thirty-eight yet-unknown-to-me leaders for a
gathering where I shared with them the harsh realities of our church's
spiritual and financial condition as well as to pitch a new vision for
the future of our congregation. That night, we prayed about our future and collected an offering of more than $20,000. We began the
long journey of defeating the fear-inducing giants of spiritual death
and devilish debt.

For nearly three decades, our church has had to face many new
giants, such as the agonizing pain of a staff member's moral failure,
the crushing weight of a pending foreclosure on a property, the para-

lyzing impact of a global pandemic, and the excruciating division over politics, race, and denominational schism. In every one of these challenges as a leader, I've had to remember back to our "valley of Elah" when I saw God kill that giant of fear in my first days as a pastor. I knew that the same God who took care of us decades ago would take care of us now. The old Gospel song says, "He never failed me yet." We serve the God who saw us through then and will see us through now! That's what helped David out of the cave of fear, and it can help us out of ours too.

Who's in the Cave with Me?

In 2019, I went on a mission trip to Kenya. There I was able to reconnect with Harrison, a Kenyan leader whom I first met at my church years earlier during his trip to America. Harrison is a remarkable follower of Jesus. When he visited in 2016, my wife, Cheryl, and I hosted him and several other African leaders in our home. In 2019, I ate in his home in Kenya. Harrison said this to me. "Jorge, there is a saying in the Kikuyu tribe, 'Friendship is steps. If I see my steps in your house and your steps in mine, then we are friends.'" Friendship, companionship, community all require steps. Steps are investment. We were made for this by God.

You see, the first crisis in the Bible was not the whole fruit eating incident with Adam, Eve, and the tempting snake. This was a moral crisis. The first crisis in the Bible was a relational crisis when God observed Adam and said, "It is not good that the man should be alone." (Genesis 2:18). The "not good" of aloneness is especially true when we are afraid. When we are afraid, we need others to help us through. We need friends to join us in our cave of fear.

David may have entered the cave of Adullam alone, but he was soon to have some company. Look at 1 Samuel 22:1b-2:

When his brothers and all his father's house heard of it, they went down there to him. Everyone who was in distress, and everyone who was in debt, and everyone who was discontented gathered to him; and he became captain over them. Those who were with him numbered about four hundred.

We've all heard the phrase, "Misery loves company." But this crew with David in the cave had a bad case of advanced misery. In general, two groups joined the fearful soon-to-be King, his family, and a ragtag group of others.

Remember David's family? The author calls them "his brothers and all his father's house." These were the seven not-chosen ones and the relatives of his dad who saw David as so insignificant that he left David unnamed and unnumbered earlier in life. There is nothing as crazy as family. Benjamin Franklin famously said that guests, like fish, begin to smell after three days. It is truer of family. Yet, David welcomes his dysfunctional family onto his team.

But look who else joins in. The author describes them this way: Everyone who was in distress, and everyone who was in debt, and everyone who was discontented gathered to him. A word study of the Hebrew meanings of these descriptions reveals more about these three groups of people who joined David. Here's what we learn. Those "in distress" describe people who are under stress, as when a city is under siege with enemies closing in around them, crushing them on all sides. These are people in "anguished pressure." Talk about fear! The phrase "in debt" is used for people with more than just money troubles. The word *nashaw* describes a person who has gone astray morally as well. The *discontented*, or *mar nefesh* in Hebrew, is a description of people who harbor bitter, angry souls.

This crew needs therapy, spiritual direction, and financial planning. Where is the character, competency, and chemistry in this sad lot? Where are all the level 5 leaders in this posse? Why didn't David take a spiritual gifts inventory to find those with the leadership gifts to join his team? These are the bottom feeders, the people nobody else wants or sees. These were not first round draft picks. What a motley crew! David's cave companions were a bunch of people in distress, in debt, and discontented. This is a cave full of fear-filled "misfit toys"! That's who I want on my team (tongue in cheek).

If you read the rest of the story, you will find that many of this ragamuffin crew by God's grace and mercy becomes the group who are decades later called "David's Mighty Men." In part 2 of Samuel's books near the end of David's life, the author calls many of these "cave dwellers," David's "mighty warriors." 2 Samuel 23:8a (NIV) says, "*These are the names of David's mighty warriors.*" They would be the ones who would be with him when David eventually becomes the king of Israel. David's leadership team was built not in a castle but a cave, a cave of fear. Through this common experience of fear, God formed a mighty community of faith.

The team members formed in the caves of Adullum would become mighty warriors over time. Days and nights of strategizing for battles, surviving fighting within the ranks, and conflict on the theatre of war would galvanize this mess of humanity into mighty warriors. It kind of reminds me of a story I heard about an itinerating Rabbi from nowhere Nazareth who gathered around him a ragtag group of adolescents and a handful of women who eventually changed the world! It also reminds me of the sage words of Paul in 1 Corinthians 1:26-31 (NIV):

> Brothers and sisters, think of what you were when you were called. Not many of you were wise by human standards; not many were influential; not many were of noble birth. But God chose the foolish things of the world to shame the wise; God chose the weak things of the world to shame the strong. God chose the lowly things of this world and the despised things—and the things that are not—to nullify the things that are, so that no one may boast before him. It is because of him that you are in Christ Jesus, who has become

for us wisdom from God—that is, our righteousness, holiness and redemption. Therefore, as it is written: "Let the one who boasts boast in the Lord."

It seems to me that God's leadership strategy is to choose the least likely people to do God's bidding so that in the end, God gets all the credit.

There is a powerful story in the first book of the Bible about two feuding twin brothers, Jacob and Esau (Genesis 25-35). After a series of poor decisions by the older brother, Esau, and fiendish and manipulative actions by the younger brother, Jacob, they part ways. Jacob leaves his family of origin literally worried that his big brother would kill him. Years later, by the grace of God, they reconcile. The Bible describes beautifully the moment they see one another for the first time in years. With a gift in hand and a heart of reconciliation, the once-devious younger brother Jacob says to his older brother, Esau, "And what a relief to see your friendly smile. It is like seeing the face of God!" (Genesis 33:10)

This the presence and the power of God at work in community. It is seeing the face of God in the face of another. This was true for Jacob and Esau. It was true for David and his mighty men and it's been true for me too.

I've been in a pastor's group for more than thirty years. Matthew, Dale, Max, Wayne, Joe, and Doug have been my band of brothers who have stuck with me through the years. This misfit, ragtag covenant group has been my lifeline. They stood with me through the fearful decade of hell during my son's addiction. They've helped me navigate fearful decisions about our ministry at Grace Church. They've challenged me on my fearful hurts, habits, and hang-ups and then walked with me through my recovery. I wouldn't be a pastor and likely not even in ministry if it weren't for these guys. It's not good to be alone especially during fearful times.

Finding Refuge in God

The problem with fear is that it can lead us to try to hide from others. Worse yet, we can even try to hide from God. This impulse in us goes all the way back to the earliest pages of the Bible. Remember after eating the fruit from the tree at the center of the Garden of Eden, Adam and Eve hid themselves, because as Adam told God, "I was afraid!" (Genesis 3:10). Fear does this to us. It leaves us feeling exposed, and our response is to try to hide. The further we run into hiding from God, the more fear will have a hold on us.

Though at first David hides in the cave fearful of Saul and his army, he eventually allows his cave of fear to be transformed. Eventually, he gets very honest about his fears. David used his cave time to face his fears. In doing so, he encountered God. We know this because from this dark place, David penned a prayer. Look with me at a prayer of David's that he wrote while in this very cave. It's found in Psalm 142:5-7.

> I cry to you, O Lord; I say, 'You are my refuge, my portion in the land of the living.' Listen to my cry, for I am brought very low. Save me from my persecutors, for they are too strong for me. Bring me out of prison, so that I may give thanks to your name. The righteous will surround me, for you will deal bountifully with me.

In a very "low" place that he calls a "prison," David declares that God is his refuge. A refuge is a sanctuary and a shelter. A refuge is a haven and a home. A refuge is a place of protection and a place of peace. Only God can turn a "prison" into a "refuge."

One of my mentors was the Rev. Dr. J. Howard Olds. He was a masterful preacher. Much of his power in proclaiming God's Word came from his own journey of suffering through a dozen years of cancer, which eventually took his life at the age of 62. When describing the valleys he had been through in life, he once said, "Some valleys are too vast to go over, too deep to tunnel under, and too wide to go around. The only choice is to go through the valley."

This was where I found myself during times of ordeals. I saw no escape. I had to face my fears. When I asked, "Where does my help come from?" the answer that I found was as old as the words of David himself in Psalm 121: "My help comes from the Lord!" When I took my fears to the Lord, something indescribable began to occur. My prison of fears was transformed into a refuge of faith.

What is faith? Faith is simply defined as trust. Using a mustard seed of trust in my prayers and pain, God turned my prison of fear into a refuge of faith. The words of Irish poet and preacher Joseph Medlicott Scriven came alive for me in my cave of fear. He wrote some words you may have sung before:

Are we weak and heavy-laden,
Cumbered with a load of care?
Precious Savior, still our refuge—
Take it to the Lord in prayer;
Do thy friends despise, forsake thee?
Take it to the Lord in prayer;
In His arms He'll take and shield thee,
Thou wilt find a solace there.[12]

Jesus . . . he's our refuge. Another song by Danilo Montero, in my native tongue from Puerto Rico, affirms this promise: "*Dulce refugio en la tormenta es Jesucristo el Salvador*. Sweet shelter in the storm is Jesus Christ the Savior."[13] Jesus is our refuge in the storms of life. No matter what language you speak, no matter what pain you bear, Jesus is your refuge. If you are in a cave of fear, Jesus will meet you there.

---

12. Joseph Medlicott Scriven, *What a Friend We Have in Jesus* (n.p., 1855).
13. Frank Giraldo, *Dulce Refugio* (Grupo Canzion Editora, 1997).

Let me ask you a question. In whom or in what do you find your refuge? Is your refuge in your spouse? I hope not. He or she is going to let you down. Is your refuge in your job? I hope not. It will end someday. Is your refuge in your money? Jesus said we couldn't have it both ways and love God and money. Your refuge isn't in the government, the schools, or even the church. Your refuge isn't in the president, a teacher, or your pastor. Nothing and nobody but God can be our place of refuge. David knows this. That's why David says to God, "You are my place of refuge!"

Have you ever prayed like that? "God, you are my refuge." Say that prayer right now. "God, you are my refuge." Now, think of your fears. What are you afraid of today? What is it that is keeping you up at night? What fear makes you angry, makes you crazy, makes you want to hide, makes you want to fight, makes you want to flee, or that causes you to freeze in fear? Now, pray that prayer that David taught us. "God, you are my refuge." Pray it as many times as you need to until you can see God before you offering you hope, relief, and peace.

Heart Shaping in the Cave of Fear

Both Samuel in the Old Testament (1 Samuel 13:14) and Paul in the New Testament (Acts 13:22) called David "a man after God's own heart." Could it be that his time in the cave of fear helped shape his God-pursuing heart? If you find yourself in a cave of fear, you are in great company. David teaches us from his cave of fear that when we enter this dark place we can

- remember God's deliverance in the past,
- gather in community, and
- find refuge in God.

These practices cultivate the space we need to overcome our fear, for as Paul wrote in Philippians 4:7, "the peace of God, which surpasses all understanding" will "guard your hearts and your minds in Christ Jesus." The word that we translate *guard* literally means "to guard, protect by a military guard, either to prevent hostile invasion, or to keep the inhabitants of a besieged city from flight."[14] Using your sanctified imagination, think of huge Roman guards stationed around your heart, the center of your emotions, and your mind, the center of your intellect, protecting you from fearful feelings and thoughts. This is God's promise. This is finding God in the cave of fear.

This is what David experienced in Adullam. It's the fear-chasing presence and power of God. In the Gospels of Matthew, Mark, and Luke, each writer tells the story of Jesus and his disciples being in a boat when a storm arose.[15] Having traveled to Israel on several occasions, I have seen a huge windstorm peak over the mountains surrounding the water churning it violently. In all three accounts, Jesus is asleep in the middle of a great storm in the Sea of Galilee. The image of Jesus asleep in the storm is one way to consider how God acts when we are overwhelmed by fear. But in the story, Jesus awakens and calms the storm. Sometimes, this is the way God calms our fears. His presence supernaturally settles the fearful tempest in our soul.

In John's story about the disciples in a boat during a storm, Jesus isn't even in the boat.[16] Instead Jesus walks on the water to them. John 6:19-20 reports it this way: "They had rowed three or four miles when suddenly they saw Jesus walking on the water toward the boat. They were terrified, but he called out to them, 'Don't be afraid. I am here!' Then they were eager to let him in the boat, and immediately they arrived at their destination!" I love this image of

---

14. The Greek Bible, www.greekbible.com/l.php?froure/w_v_3fai-s--_accessed 11/30/2022.
15. Matthew 8:23–27; Mark 4:36–41; and Luke 8:22–25.
16. John 6:16-21.

Jesus and storms too. Here, Jesus walks into our fearful situations. The storms are still lapping over into our lives but it's OK because Jesus is with us.

In my research, I discovered there is a phobia named astraphobia. It's the fear of storms. Our second grandchild, Levi, might have this one. When he was a toddler, he was with us often when our Florida summer storms would quickly descend upon us. The thunder and lightning can be violent. Levi would run into our arms shouting, "Dunder, Grandpa. Dunder!" I'd hold him close whispering words of solace and security. "It's all right, Levi. Grandpa has you. It's going to be all right." These are the words our heavenly Father whispers to us in our cave of fear.

Chapter 3: With Elijah in the Cave of Depression

Long enough, God—
you've ignored me long enough.
I've looked at the back of your head
long enough. Long enough
I've carried this ton of trouble,
lived with a stomach full of pain.
Long enough my arrogant enemies
have looked down their noses at me.
—Psalm 13:1-2 (THE MESSAGE)

Depression is like dread being stuck on a spin cycle.
—Wes Olds

My wife, Cheryl, is the only child of two amazing, hardworking mid-Westerners from Indiana. They deeply love Jesus and the church and raised their only daughter to imitate them. Her parents also loved each other and her. Their home was very quiet and peaceful. Think *Little House on the Prairie*. For the younger readers, Google it! In their quiet and peaceful home, getting mad, arguing, and disagreeing with authority was unheard of, and conflict was not allowed.

One of the negative results of this kind of home environment for Cheryl was that she was deeply concerned about "what the neighbors thought." Tucking negative thoughts deeply into her heart and mind damaged her soul as she aged. Imagine the "shock" to her system when she married me. Think of "My Big Fat Greek Wedding." Again, Google it. I grew up in a loud Latino family where the person who yelled the loudest and the longest won the fight. Sharing her thoughts and feelings with me especially in the early days of our marriage was almost impossible. Given my undiagnosed dry drunk propensities to anger in my twenties and her undiagnosed codependency, you can see that our marriage was set up for some major struggles.

Pete Scazzero famously said, "Jesus may live in your heart, but grandpa lives in your bones."[17] By the grace of God, over the forty-plus years of our marriage, both of us have healed many of our family of origin wounds but not without challenges both deep within ourselves and in our relationships. For one, as our youngest son's addiction escalated, Cheryl entered a cave of depression. Like a snowball gaining speed and density, Nathan's addiction to opiates became so forceful that we could no longer chalk it up to simple adolescent pushback to parental authority. That shipped had sailed. Our denial smashed against the hard and obvious rocks of yet another round of arrests and incarceration. I got mad. Cheryl got codependent, and it left her in a dark place. Would she hide or would she heal in her cave of depression?

Depression Defined

What is depression? I know that in the past, I have cavalierly said, "I'm feeling a bit depressed today," sadly minimizing the deep dread of a person who really struggles with clinical depression the

---

17. Pete Scazzero, *The Emotionally Healthy Leader* (Grand Rapids, MI: Zondervan, 2015), 72.

way my wife, Cheryl, did, as well as my lifelong ministry colleague Wes. It was Wes, trying to help me really understand clinical depression, who said to me, "Jorge, depression is like dread being stuck on a spin cycle." This really helped me gain some sympathy for what he, my wife, and countless other family and friends experience on a daily basis. Many just can't "get over it." According to Mayo Clinic, "Depression ranges in seriousness from mild, temporary episodes of sadness to severe, persistent depression. Clinical depression is the more-severe form of depression, also known as major depression or major depressive disorder. Clinical depression can affect people of any age, including children. However, clinical depression symptoms, even if severe, usually improve with psychological counseling, antidepressant medications, or a combination of the two."[18]

As Mayo confirms, every human being goes through seasons, sometime short and sometime long, that we would put under the category of "mild, temporary episodes of sadness." In 2013, I was given a four-month sabbatical by the leaders of Grace Church. It was the first time in twenty-nine years of active ministry that I had taken any extended time completely unplugged from my work in the church. Upon returning, a planned shift in my leadership responsibilities occurred that really messed with my identity as a pastor. This coupled with being totally disconnected from the ministry for four months left me in one of these extended seasons of depression. That fall, in a moment of confession, through tears, I seriously uttered to my closest friends, "I think I might be depressed." I engaged with our family therapist for a season, asked my covenant group of more than twenty years at the time to hold me accountable to a regimen of healing, and by the grace of God, my "mild episode of sadness" passed.

---

18. Daniel K Hall-Flavin, MD, "Clinical Depression: What Does That Mean?," Mayo Clinic (Mayo Foundation for Medical Education and Research, May 13, 2017), http://www.mayoclinic.org/diseases-conditions/depression/expert-answers/clinical-depression/faq-20057770.

For my wife, Cheryl, her journey of depression is more accurately described by Mayo's definition, "Clinical depression is the more-severe form of depression, also known as major depression or major depressive disorder." I asked her to share her journey with clinical depression here:

> I was diagnosed with depression and anxiety in the fall of 2006. It was a shock to me and everyone that knew me. My nickname is "Smiley," due to my positive outlook and bouncy personality. At forty-three years old, I had a strong marriage and deep friendships. My two sons were eighteen and twenty-three at that time. I loved Jesus and served him in public school and at church.
>
> What did I have to be depressed about? My life looked perfect! As an only child I learned to hide my "negative emotions" and make my outward actions/appearances "positive" to the "neighbors." My parents never argued in front of me. My childhood home was peaceful and calm. Somehow, I learned deep down that what others thought of me was very important.
>
> In August of 2006, my youngest son was arrested yet again. The previous arrests of shoplifting, larceny, and drug possession had been expunged by his generous grandparents and the private criminal attorney we hired. We tried to save him from himself and his bad decisions by sending him to a counselor and wiping his criminal record clean.
>
> Now as an eighteen-year-old senior in high school, he was arrested again. Another felony. Nathan was a senior at the same school I was a teacher. I loved seeing him as the school news broadcaster, but now I was embarrassed and believed it was my fault. I felt I was a failure as his mom.
>
> On the outside I was trying to hold it together at work, at home, and at church. But inwardly, I was jumping at every phone call and late-night knock on the door. I would

get lost while driving to my regular locations in town and have panic attacks before school and at bedtime. Sleep was a joke. My heart would race for hours when I lay down. I'd walk throughout the dark house, afraid of what the next day might hold. I was mortified that my coworkers and church friends would find out.

On Halloween, I broke down at school and told the principal my struggles. I needed a few days off because I couldn't stop crying. It was impossible to hide my nervousness from my students. So, I took the next five days off, got the keys to my friend's beach condo and made appointments with a counselor every day that week. It was like I was watching myself go through the motions as I packed food and clothes and pulled out of the driveway just as the trick-or-treaters were starting to make their rounds. At the beach, the counselor had me journal daily about my disappointments and anger. I never knew I was so mad!

Perhaps my depression was situational, but after decades of stuffing my anger, it was overwhelming. My counselor explained that depression is also fueled by inward anger. "Smiley" couldn't smile or sing praise songs. I was drowning in shame and self-condemnation as a mother. I felt helpless to protect my son. I had no words to explain this to my husband. Intimacy was difficult, because when I'd relax, I'd sob. I had no energy. I had to force myself out of bed, out of the house, and to church. To focus was very hard. I would forget the year, the date, and simple words in conversation. It was scary. I was embarrassed.

The medical doctor helped by prescribing medications for depression, anxiety, and sleep. The medication helped me to not sob and be able to "somewhat" function at school. I could sleep with Ambien. I could function without panic attacks while using Xanax. My moods were more stabilized with Zoloft. During the next eleven years of Nathan's roller coaster of sobriety and relapse, criminal activity, and struggling to find employment as a felon, I chose to change my response.

I started with a small group that studied the *Boundaries* book by Henry Cloud.[19] I learned that it wasn't healthy for me to be responsible for anyone but me. I could not control or fix my son or his situation. It was none of my business what others thought of me. God loves and accepts me. I needed to focus on how God sees me. It wasn't easy because codependency ran deep in my bones, but fixing and over-helping was injuring me and my son.

During one of Nathan's residential rehab stints, the parents were required to attend classes for loved ones of addicts. Al-Anon worked for me. The devotional guides were like no devotional I'd ever done. Then I started attending the Celebrate Recovery program at our church. I participated in a STEP study three times. (STEP studies are when you go through the 12 steps of Alcoholics Anonymous with a small accountability group.) These were the things God used to heal me.

As Cheryl's spouse, I have had a front row seat to her life transformation. It's real and bone deep. Cheryl spent time in a cave of depression. It was not only a holy place where she met with God but became a healing place to learn how to manage her depression.

From Mountaintop to Valley

Two prominent miracle workers of note in the Old Testament mirror the wonder working and supernatural power we see in Jesus in the four Gospel narratives. The first is Moses. He's the ten plagues, Red Sea–parting, water-and-quail providing miracle worker who led

---

19.   Henry Cloud and John Townsend, *Boundaries: When to Say Yes, When to Say No to Take Control of Your Life* (Grand Rapids, MI: Zondervan, 2017).

God's enslaved people from Pharaoh's Egypt to the Promised Land filled with milk and honey.

The other great Old Testament miracle worker is Elijah, the prophet of God whom we meet in 1 Kings 17 when he tells an impoverished widow that her jars of flour and bottle of oil will not run out during an extended drought and then later raises this same widow's son from the dead (1 Kings 17). This colorful man of God is the messy biblical character with whom we will enter a cave of depression. You don't often think about this kind of spiritual superstar wrestling with the blues, but sure enough he does.

Being a prophet in the Old Testament was no fun. Just look at how most prophets were treated. No ancient Israelite kid ever grew up saying, "You know, when I grow up, I don't want to be a policeman or firefighter. I want to be a prophet!" Being a prophet meant wandering around aimlessly, being called a lunatic and a killjoy, saying things that people really didn't want to hear, and constantly second-guessing yourself. Oh yeah, and often you got killed!

Elijah lived during a time in Israel's history when it must have felt like the wheels were coming off the bus for God's chosen people. Israel was ruled by a horrible, evil king named Ahab who married a Canaanite woman named Jezebel and she was even worse than he was. To top it off, the Israelites turned away from their God, Yahweh, and started worshiping the pagan god Baal and a goddess named Asherah. One day, God sent the prophet Elijah to confront the evil king Ahab with this message, "As surely as God lives, the God of Israel before whom I stand in obedient service, the next years are going to see a total drought – not a drop of dew or rain unless I say otherwise." (1 Kings 17:1b)

This didn't make King Ahab or his wife Queen Jezebel happy, and when Jezebel gets unhappy, the Bible says that she becomes *cra-cra*. That's street lingo for "livid." This is when Elijah immediately hears God giving him this second command, "Then the Lord said to

Elijah, 'Go to the east and hide.'" (1 Kings 17:2a). Elijah spends the next three years in hiding, until God sends him back to the king with a proposal for a winner-take-all battle royal to see whose God is the mightiest. In 1 Kings 18:19-23, Elijah challenges the King and his false prophets with these fighting words:

> Summon all Israel to join me at Mount Carmel, along with the 450 prophets of Baal and the 400 prophets of Asherah who are supported by Jezebel...[and] bring two bulls. The prophets of Baal may choose whichever one they wish and cut it into pieces and lay it on the wood of their altar, but without setting fire to it. Then call on the name of your god, and I will call on the name of the Lord. The god who answers by setting fire to the wood is the true God! And all the people agreed.

Sure enough, hundreds of thousands, maybe even millions, of Israelites assembled on the Carmel mountain range to watch the battle between the prophets of Baal and Asherah and the prophet of Yahweh. The prophets of Baal and Asherah won the coin toss, and Elijah elected to defer to the second half, so they started praying and dancing and singing to the god Baal . . . but, nothing! Not a spark or a flicker. Absolutely nothing. At one point, Elijah starts to trash talk: At noon Elijah began to taunt them. "Shout louder!" he said. "Surely he is a god! Perhaps he is deep in thought, or busy, or traveling. Maybe he is sleeping and must be awakened" (1 Kings 18:27). The Hebrew for "deep in thought" actually is a euphemism for relieving yourself. Perhaps Baal is "going poop!" says the man of God. Don't you just love the Bible? Straight up, Old Testament prophet smack-talk! More praying, dancing, and singing by the prophets of Baal ensued, but still no fire.

Now it was Elijah's turn, but first he does something strange. He asks them to soak everything with water, the altar, the ox meat, even the firewood not once but three times. Then Elijah prays to Yahweh.

Fire immediately falls from heaven and burns up the offering. All the people see it happen and fall on their faces in worship, exclaiming, "God is the true God! God is the true God!" Winner . . . Elijah and his God!

Wow! What a story! And that's where it ends . . . when we tell it at children's church. The next part says that Elijah instructed the people to seize all of the false prophets and kill them. Apparently, Elijah hadn't read my chapter about the "Cave of Anger!" And then the real miracle happens. Elijah prays for rain, and after three years of drought the rain comes pouring down. Elijah, the hunted and hated prophet, has now become the hero whom God has used to literally save their lives. He has defeated 950 false prophets, led Israel to repentance, and managed to call both fire and rain down from heaven. Not too shabby. At this point, you might expect the TV cameras to pan over to Elijah who, after receiving the Super Bowl MVP award shouts, "I'm going to Disney World!" But that's not exactly what happens.

Elijah Enters His Cave of Depression

I love the messy spirituality of the Bible. It does not candy coat or excuse away the struggle real people of faith have in navigating the challenges of life. What happens next to Elijah is far from a "happily ever after" ending. With the glow of victory all over Elijah, the biblical narrative tells what happened to the Most Valuable Prophet next:

> Now Ahab told Jezebel everything Elijah had done and how he had killed all the prophets with the sword. So Jezebel sent a messenger to Elijah to say, "May the gods deal with me, be it ever so severely, if by this time tomorrow I do not make your life like that of one of them." Elijah was afraid and ran for his life. When he came to Beersheba in Judah, he left his servant there, while he himself went a day's journey into the wilderness. He came to a broom bush, sat down under

it and prayed that he might die. "I have had enough, Lord," he said. "Take my life; I am no better than my ancestors." Then he lay down under the bush and fell asleep. (1 Kings 19:1-5a NIV)

What?

Wait! Elijah just took out 950 false prophets with fire from heaven and he's afraid of the King's wife? Elijah the hero just went from a literal mountaintop moment in his life to hiding under a broom bush, scared, exhausted, and in despair. *He even prays that he might die.* This guy is depressed! Elijah lets his fear and exhaustion drive him into hiding, and ultimately it takes him all the way to a literal dark place. 1 Kings 19:9a puts a GPS on Elijah. "There he went into a cave and spent the night." Elijah was in a cave of depression.

Making It Out of the Cave of Depression

I'm calling Elijah's cave the "cave of depression," but I want to be careful with that term again. When I say *depression* here, I'm not talking about clinical depression, which is a mental and emotional condition that requires medical treatment and therapy to address its underlying causes, which include things like brain chemistry and our DNA. For the readers who struggle with clinical depression, my wife's testimony is for you. Please see your doctor. Find a good therapist and supplement your treatment with other resources like recovery and prayer ministries.

There is no evidence that Elijah was clinically depressed. His seems more situational. My dear friend Kevin Griffin calls it "Elijah feeling the broom bush blues!" Have you ever been there? We all have. Everybody does some depression cave time at some point in their lives, not just Elijah. Several of the most famous people in the Bible entered the cave of depression:

- Moses, after he has led the Israelites out of Egypt, when he asked God to kill him.

- David, after being hunted by King Saul, when he hid in a cave in despair.

- Peter, after he denied he knew Jesus three times and wept bitterly.

- The disciples, after Jesus was crucified and they locked themselves in a secret room.

- Paul, after the people turned against him and he wrote that it might be better if he died.

- Even Jesus himself, after the Last Supper, said in the Garden of Gethsemane that his soul was being crushed to the point of death.

We all do some depression cave time! Just like Elijah, we often find ourselves headed to the cave of depression not long after the rush of an adrenaline-fueled high.

The Gospels tell us about Jesus being baptized in the Jordan River, and it's amazing, complete with a dove and a voice from heaven! Guess what happens immediately after that spiritual high? "Then Jesus was led by the Spirit into the wilderness to be tempted there by the devil. For forty days and forty nights he fasted and became very hungry. During that time the devil came and said to him." (Matthew 4:1-3a NLT). Apparently, the devil knows when we're at our most vulnerable moments, when we are physically, emotionally, and spiritually in want. Life can toss us into a cave of depression, but then our adversary will do everything he can to keep us in there! But we don't have to stay there. Elijah's story helps us when we enter into our unique cave of depression.

In the cave of depression, the darkness can become so dark that it blinds us to possibility in our lives. The sadness can become so pervasive that making simple, everyday decisions, such as getting out of bed, showering, getting dressed, and eating breakfast seem overwhelming. In the cave of depression, reading the Bible to hear from God or engaging in times of intimate prayer may seem impossible. In terms of relationships, engaging in simple conversation and especially healthy conflict are outside of one's reach. The cave of depression is dark and isolated.

Restoring Rhythms

While Elijah sinks into his cave of depression, God meets with the sad and scared prophet. As you read what the *messenger* from God says to the *depressed man* of God, notice what phrase appears twice:

> All at once an angel touched him and said, "Get up and eat." He looked around, and there by his head was some bread baked over hot coals, and a jar of water. He ate and drank and then lay down again. The angel of the Lord came back a second time and touched him and said, "Get up and eat, for the journey is too much for you." So, he got up and ate and drank. Strengthened by that food, he traveled forty days and forty nights until he reached Horeb, the mountain of God. (1 Kings 19:5b-8)

Did you catch it? It's the command from the angel to "Get up and eat."

Why did the angel have to say it the second time? For the same reason Cheryl and I had to tell our teenage sons 30 million times to get up for school, do their homework, take a bath, brush their teeth, and put on underwear. They never got it the first time. Neither did Elijah. So, twice God's messenger had to tell the prophet to get a bite to eat. You see, the cave of depression sucks all of the energy out of you and makes you want to lie down and hide. This is why God prompts Elijah to do the exact opposite: get up and eat! Notice what God doesn't tell him to do:

- "Snap out of it!" (By the way, please don't ever say this to someone who's depressed.)
- "Don't worry, be happy!"
- "If you were a good prophet, you wouldn't feel this way!"

God prompts Elijah to choose what it is healthy and normal in the midst of his discouragement. God practically and simply invites the bewildered and beleaguered prophet to reengage with his normal routines. "Get up and eat man of God." What might "Get up and eat" mean for contemporary people? How about this?

- Pay the bills.
- Read the kids a bedtime story.
- Wake up in the morning and go to work.
- Go to church.
- Pray. . . . If it seems too hard to, simply say, "Dear God, It's too hard to pray right now. Please help me. Amen."
- Call a friend.
- Go to your small group.
- Bless somebody who's not expecting it.
- Serve someone in need.

Elijah's first step was literally taking the first step. Get up and eat.

One of my dear friends told me that his counselor taught him that when he's caught in the cave of depression, he needs to have an "opposite day." If the cave tells him to stay in bed he must do the opposite. He has to get up, shower, eat, and start his day. When the cave tells him not to pray he needs to do the opposite—break out his journal and write out some prayers. We need to restore our rhythms to make it through the cave of depression. God meets us more than halfway, as he did with Elijah, but we must take responsibility for our choices. I'm the only one who can choose to cooperate with Grace. Dallas Willard masterfully wrote in his book *The Great Omission*, "Grace is not opposed to effort, it is opposed to earning. Earning is an attitude. Effort is an action. Grace, you know, does not just have to do with forgiveness of sins alone."[20] We need to put in the effort to restore our rhythms as depression lures us into inactivity.

Reclaiming Identity

The journey out of our cave of depression is not an automatic one. I love that immediately after Elijah gets up and eats, he runs off and hides in another cave on Mt. Horeb. But God isn't finished with him yet. In this new cave, God asks Elijah a question: "What are you doing here, Elijah?" (1 Kings 19:9b). "What are you doing in this second cave still running and hiding, Elijah?" Elijah honestly responds with, "I have zealously served the Lord God Almighty. But the people of Israel have broken their covenant with you, torn down your altars, and killed every one of your prophets. I am the only one left, and now they are trying to kill me, too" (1 Kings 19:10). I notice two things about us when we are overwhelmed with life's struggles that Elijah's response to God illustrates.

First is our propensity to focus on what we do for God over what God has done for us. In his bluesy state, the prophet *of* God informs God of all that he is doing *for* God. Catch the irony? "Can't you see all the great stuff I alone am doing for you God?" Lost in his report to God here is the confidence he has in his relationship with God, which we saw on Mt. Carmel when Elijah took on the prophets of Baal and Asherah in the name of God. On Mount Carmel, it was all

---

20. Dallas Willard, *The Great Omission* (San Francisco, CA: HarperOne, 2014), 61, 80.

about God. In the cave of Mt. Horeb, it was all about Elijah: "Prone to wander, Lord I feel it. Prone to leave the God I love."[21]

Second, in the cave of depression, we have a propensity to come down with a bad case of "terminal uniqueness." Terminal uniqueness is when we wrongly believe that out of the billions of people on the planet who are currently living, we are the *only* ones going through our sorrows and sufferings. This is where Elijah was and where many of us are now living. Whenever I find myself in that place, my wife Cheryl tells me that I'm stricken with a case of PLOM disease: Poor Little, Old Me!

Grace meets us where we are, not where we need to be. God's grace met this worn thin, depressed champion, Elijah, right where he was, with Elijah's focus on himself. From the bottom of his cave of depression, the only place the depleted prophet could look was up. God commands Elijah to get out of the cave and go stand on the mountain called "the mountain of God," for God's presence was going to force Elijah from his cave. The biblical narrative is epic:

> And as Elijah stood there, the Lord passed by, and a mighty windstorm hit the mountain. It was such a terrible blast that the rocks were torn loose, but the Lord was not in the wind. After the wind there was an earthquake, but the Lord was not in the earthquake. And after the earthquake there was a fire, but the Lord was not in the fire. And after the fire there was the sound of a gentle whisper. When Elijah heard it, he wrapped his face in his cloak and went out and stood at the entrance of the cave. (1 Kings 19:11b-13)

Three cataclysmic natural events happen right in front of the weary warrior. A windstorm, an earthquake, and a fire appear, but the text is clear. God's presence and voice were not in any of these mighty acts. Could it be that God wanted to right-size Elijah's self-importance after Elijah had been the instrument of God's mighty

---

21.   Robert Robertson, *Come Thou Fount of Every Blessing*, 1759.

acts defeating the 950 false prophets? Had Elijah gotten a bit "big for his britches"? Did he need a little air let out of his big head? I'm not sure, but the contrast between the grandness of the three natural events where God was not and the gentleness of God's whisper seems more than coincidental.

I know in my life as a pastor, there have been moments of adrenaline-pumping ministry in which everything I and my teams did seemed to be going right. These were our "defeating the false prophet, fire-from-heaven moments." Here's a dirty little preacher secret. The two big things measured in ministry are "butts and bucks": how many people come to worship, how much money is coming in. In my denomination, an annual report is released noting the twenty-five fastest growing churches in America. No pastor would dare wish that their church be on that list, right? For several years, the church I serve was on that list, and for a few of those years we were number 1. "We're number 1!" . . . Can you hear Freddy singing, "We are the champions my friends?"[22] But here's my truth. When we fell off the list, I became depressed. It's sick. I know—my value had become attached to my performance. I know I'm not terminally unique here. It can happen for the stay-at-home mom who lives vicariously through her kids' performance in school or sports. It can happen to the over-achieving employee striving for the next rung on the ladder of success. And sadly, it can happen to the over-functioning pastor.

You see, as God whispered to the depressed Elijah, God was not interested in Elijah's spiritual resume. It seems to me that God was helping Elijah reclaim his identity as a child of God and a person of worth. God's presence was in the "gentle whisper." The Hebrew word used here literally translates to the word "silence." When he was depressed following an adrenaline-filled episode doing God's mission, God met Elijah in the silence.

---

22. Brian May, "We Will Rock You." (Elektra. 1977).

Practices for Depressed People

The Greek philosopher Socrates famously said, "The unexamined life is not worth living."[23] This is the wisdom of the Bible too. Paul gave Timothy, the young pastor of the fledgling church in Ephesus, this sage advice, *Keep a close watch on how you live* (1 Timothy 4:16a). This is an invitation for all followers of Jesus to perform an honest evaluation of their lives, including their relationship with God, themselves, and others. Put more simply, it's the command in scripture to love God and love neighbor as we love ourselves.

It's been said that we need to be careful and watchful over our soul when we are hungry, angry, lonely, or tired (HALT). This phrase finds its origins in the recovery program of Alcoholics Anonymous.[24] Its wisdom echoes Paul's admonition in 1 Corinthians 10:12 (NIV): "So, if you think you are standing firm, be careful that you don't fall!" For me, I have two practices at the beginning and end of my day that help me listen to God's "gentle whisper."

My morning practice is a Bible reading and reflection time in which I journal the whisper of the Spirit for my life.[25] This 30- to 45-minute-long exercise has sharpened my ear to God's gentle whisper more than any other discipline. I have observed in my life and the lives of others that daily Bible engagement more than any other practice helps Christ followers grow in their faith.

My evening practice is a time for self-reflection or what some call "the daily examen."[26] For my nighttime ritual, I simply review my day and ask the Holy Spirit to help me accurately assess my re-

---

23.   Plato, *Apology*, section 38a.
24.   Susanne Reed, PhD, "How Using the Halt Concept Prevents Alcohol Relapse," Alcoholics Anonymous, March 9, 2022, http://www.alcoholicsanonymous.com/how-using-the-halt-concept-prevents-alcohol-relapse/.
25.   For some help on daily Bible engagement, look at the Grace Church Dive Deep Bible reading program at www.egracechurch.com/bible/. Also consider, Wayne Cordeiro's book *The Divine Mentor* (Grand Rapids, MI: Bethany House Publishers, 2007).
26.   "The Daily Examen," Ignatian Spirituality, October 9, 2020, http://www.ignatianspirituality.com/ignatian-prayer/the-examen/.

lationship with God, myself, and others. I typically ask myself three questions:

- Is there anything I need to celebrate?
- Is there anything I need to confess?
- Is there anything I need to change?

Sometimes this means getting up and making a note to do something in the morning or even sending a text. It's the ongoing work of keeping my heart clean and removing anything that hinders my inner world. I have experienced God in these evening times of silent reflection. The gentle whisper of God recalibrates my soul.

So, whether it's in the early morning or late evening, God's whisper is transformative. And it's the space between in the everyday-ness of life that the whisper gets lived out. I cannot tell you the number of times that something God has spoken into my heart in the early morning as I ponder scripture becomes a word for someone sitting in my office seeking counsel at 2pm. Afterward, there is a sense of God's confirmation that I am hearing from God not just for myself but for the well-being of others.

You Are Not Alone

One final observation about Elijah's episode in and out of the cave of depression can help us. Remember Elijah's bout with terminal uniqueness? God's gentle whisper confronts this unhealthy attitude in the weary prophet. After hearing God's "gentle whisper," God asks Elijah a second time, "What are you doing here, Elijah?" (1 Kings 19:13b). Once again, Elijah gives the "I've served you zealously. I'm the only faithful one left, God" speech. It's important to note that Elijah still doesn't "get it." So, God gives Elijah one more clarifying truthful word to pierce through his dark depression. In 1 Kings 19:18 (NLT), God tells Elijah, "Yet I reserve seven thousand in Israel—all whose knees have not bowed down to Baal and whose mouths have not kissed him." Elijah's dark cave of depression had convinced him that he was the only faithful one but that was not true! There were in fact thousands upon thousands of his brothers and sisters, ready to stand with God alongside him.

In order to make it through the cave of depression, not only must we reclaim our identity as children of God but also the family of God, our tribe, and our community to which we belong. One of the most fiendish dynamics of depression is that it isolates us. Elijah's journey into the cave of depression is described this way in 1 Kings 19:3-4:

> Elijah was afraid and fled for his life. He went to Beersheba, a town in Judah, and he left his servant there. Then he went on alone into the wilderness, traveling all day. He sat down under a solitary broom tree and prayed that he might die. "I have had enough, Lord," he said. "Take my life, for I am no better than my ancestors who have already died."

Elijah went alone, sat under a solitary broom tree, and asked God to end his life. Climbing into a dark cave of depression and isolation, he had quarantined himself both from his community and from God.

Yet, Jesus died not only to rescue us from the penalty and power of sin but also to give birth to this family of faith. Paul describes the Church as the Body of Christ (Romans 12:5, 1 Corinthians 10:17; 12:27, Ephesians 4:12; 5:23, Colossians 1:24). John the Revelator heard the great multitude shouting praise to God for the wedding of the Lamb, Jesus, to the Bride, the Church (Revelation 19:7). Peter calls the people of God "a chosen people," "royal priests, a holy nation, and God's very own possession" (1 Peter 2:9). When we live deeply and genuinely connected to other followers of Jesus, we are resisting the luring voice of isolation and keeping depression at bay. This is a gift not only for us but for everyone, including but not limited to our family, church, community and yes, even world.

My favorite "preacher" story about the power of community is about a father who was having a hard time getting his daughter to bed one night. They had gone through their night ritual hundreds of times. This particular night was no exception. A glass of water. A trip to the bathroom. A prayer. A hug and kiss. "Tuck me in daddy!" Over and over again it went. Frustrated, the father said to his little girl, "Sweetheart, you have to go to bed. Now when you get scared, I want you to say out loud, 'Jesus is with me. Jesus is with me.' And then you'll be OK." With a final hug and kiss, dad shut the door and went to sleep himself.

In the night a storm arose. It began to thunder, and lightning began to flash. The scared little girl remembered the advice of her dad and she said out loud, "Jesus is with me. Jesus is with me!" With that there was a loud clap of thunder and flash of lightning. In an instant, the little girl jumped out of bed, threw open her door, and ran with all her might to her parents' room. Flinging open their door with a giant leap, she jumped into their bed landing right between mommy and daddy. Dad rolled over, wiped the sleep from his eyes, and said to his little girl, "I thought I told you when you are scared to say, 'Jesus is with me.'" "I did, Daddy, I said 'Jesus is with me. Jesus is with me,' but Daddy, sometimes I needs me a Jesus with skin on!" We all do.

Elijah heard from God that he was not terminally unique. He was not alone in his fight against unrighteousness. There were seven thousand companions who had not bowed their knees to idols and who worshipped and served God with the weary prophet. There was a host of women and men, people who were "Jesus with skin on" ready to stand with him. He was not alone.

It is very important to note that after Elijah endured his protracted season in the cave of depression that the recovering prophet's first move to was invite Elisha to be his protégé (1 Kings 19:19-21). Could his journey from the adrenaline heights of defeating the prophets of Baal to the depths of dark depression because of fear for his life have taught the solitary spokesman of God that he needed at least one companion for his life?

The cave of depression is long, dark, and deep. Sometimes we journey into the abyss and are overwhelmed by the dread we encounter again and again. "It's dread stuck on a spin cycle." For many this is their experience in this dark cavern. For others, the journey into depression's cave is brief and shallow. The experience brings momentary pain but the pain still leaves a mark. Regardless of the time in the darkness, the God of Elijah sees our journey into this dark place and he guides us through the murky, shadowy abyss.

Chapter 4: With Jesus in the Cave of Temptation

"Precious, precious, precious!" Gollum cried. "My Precious! O my Precious!" And with that, even as his eyes were lifted up to gloat on his prize, he stepped too far, toppled, wavered for a moment on the brink, and then with a shriek he fell. Out of the depths came his last wail precious, and he was gone.

—J. R. R. Tolkien, The Lord of the Rings: The Return of the King

In the summer of 1998, my wife, Cheryl, and I took our two sons, Daniel age fifteen and Nathan age ten on a twenty-eight-day "Out West" extravaganza. Having borrowed my in-laws' extended camper van, we traveled from our southwest Florida paradise to some of our nation's most treasured spots. During our adventure, we lingered in many of the most beautiful national parks, including Mesa Verde, the Grand Canyon, Arches, Zion, Grand Tetons, and Yellowstone. One of our most memorable park visits was to the lesser-known Jewel Cave National Monument in Custer County, South Dakota. Cheryl wrote in our family journal of our adventure with our boys there:

We stopped at Jewel Cave and took the 1936 historical candlelight tour that was advertised as "strenuous"! We found out why they called it strenuous because we had to crawl up and down in crevices. We crawled on our hands and knees through "Tall Man's Misery," and turned sideways through "Fat Man's Misery." We only went into this 116-mile-long cave about 1/4 of a mile, but it took us 2 hours to complete. The boys both got a turn leading our group through the adventure. It was so cool—48 degrees, that is!! We enjoyed this cave tour.

Our little family discovered the joy of caving that memorable summer.

I have learned since that caving is worldwide activity. On the Travel Channel website, world traveler and photographer Lola Akinmade Åkerström helps rookie cavers with the basics of caving. She introduces the great adventure that is caving with these words:

> Nothing unleashes your inner Batman faster than spelunking—a global sport also known as caving. This increasingly popular recreational activity has you explore caves or grottos, as you walk, climb, squeeze and crawl your way through tight passages. Enthusiasts can also zip line or rappel down different cave levels, and even dive underwater!

> With spelunking you never know what you'll find around each corner while being guided by nothing more than a headlamp: Crawl spaces reveal interesting rock formations, underground streams, waterfalls, canyons and critters, such as bats.[27]

Sign me up! I'm ready for my inner Batman to be released.

27. "What You Need to Know about Spelunking," Travel Channel, http://www.travelchannel.com/interests/outdoors-and-adventure/articles/what-you-need-to-know-about-spelunking.

In sacred scripture, caves seem to hold a similar kind of adrenaline-pumping potential for the biblical characters who enter them. They become portals for real issues of life to intersect with the Almighty. In these "crawl spaces," women and men of God discover their brokenness and their beauty. Squeezing into grottos, they come face-to-face with the pain and possibilities of their lives. God seems to do some of God's best work in dark places. And no cave may provide us more amazing possibilities than the cave of temptation.

In our journey so far, we've been with Samson in the cave of anger, David in the cave of fear, and Elijah in the cave of depression. Now, we journey with Jesus into the cave of temptation. *Temptation* is a word that sometimes gets confused with "trial" or "testing." But there is an important distinction between the two. Temptation is by definition a seduction to wrongdoing. The Bible teaches that God never tempts us to do evil (James 1:13) but rather that temptation comes from our own evil desires and impulses as well as from Satan himself. Trials, on the other hand, test our character and appear to be allowed by God to come into our lives.

This illustration might help. A craftsman built the rolltop desk in my office at home where my computer rests and upon which I am writing this book. He carefully joined pieces of wood together in precise angles with screws, nails, dowels, and glue. He carefully crafted the drawers, handles, and lid. When the desk was completed, he tested it. He put it "on trial," if you will, by applying a little pressure to the joints. His desire was not to destroy the desk but to test it. But then say a demented criminal broke into my home to destroy the desk. He might pick up a hammer and demolish it. He wants to annihilate the good and careful work of the craftsman. God tests us and allows trials. He puts healthy, holy pressure on us, but Satan is a destroyer who wants to destroy God's workmanship in you.

Paul declared that as God's saved-by-faith people, we are God's handiwork. He wrote, "For we are God's masterpiece. He has created us anew in Christ Jesus, so we can do the good things he planned for us long ago" (Ephesians 2:10). The devil and evil in all its insidious forms want to destroy God's masterpiece in us so that God's good work through us is frustrated. In this chapter, we will talk about the destructive temptations of the devil and not character-building trials allowed by God. But please hear me. God forms our character in the cave of temptation. Though we stand face-to-face with evil in all its insidious forms in this cavern, God uses these seasons of temptation, even when we fall prey to them, to teach us resilience in faith and tenacity in trust.

Roots before Wings

Before going with Jesus into the cave of temptation, it's really important to look at what happened right before Jesus enters this grotto of enticement. He is baptized by his cousin John in the Jordan River. This is one of several stories that are found in the three biographies of Jesus, or Gospels, that are most alike—Matthew, Mark, and Luke. Scholars call these three biographies the Synoptic Gospels. This happens right at the beginning of Jesus' ministry when He was about thirty years of age. Luke records it this way:

> One day when the crowds were being baptized, Jesus himself was baptized. As he was praying, the heavens opened, and the Holy Spirit, in bodily form, descended on him like a dove. And a voice from heaven said, "You are my dearly loved Son, and you bring me great joy." (Luke 3:21-22 NLT)

Now there is a theological quagmire here maybe you have never thought about. If Jesus is God in the flesh and God is perfectly sinless, then why does Jesus need to be baptized? Now think with me about the revolutionary idea that God in Christ became human like all of us. We call it the "incarnation." Followers of Jesus believe that Jesus was mysteriously 100 percent God and 100 percent a human.

I'd suggest that Jesus did not get baptized to repent of and confess his sins because he was indeed sinless. Rather, Jesus was baptized to declare his intense identification with our human weakness and sin. Jesus was embodying empathy at its best. He was stepping into our world. He was becoming like us so that we might become like him.

Before entering the Temple in Jerusalem to worship, the ancient Jews would undergo a ceremony of cleansing, called a *mikvah*. Say you touched a dead body. Well, before you could go to the Temple to pray and make offerings, one of the things the Law of Moses required was for you to step into the mikvah to be cleansed. You stepped in dirty and stepped out clean. Think of Jesus' baptism as the *mikvah* practice in reverse. Jesus steps in clean into our dirty world so he might rescue and redeem our broken people and planet.

In the Greek language, Mark's Gospel uses strong words to describe what happened when Jesus was baptized. The translators of the New Living Translation of the Bible describe the event in this way: "he saw the heavens splitting apart and the Holy Spirit descending on him." Mark is the only Gospel writer to use a Greek word that doesn't just mean "open" but "tear." Mark wants us to know that God "ripped open" heaven and sent his Spirit to descend upon Jesus. This was a cosmic event of epic proportions even though it was happening in nowhere Israel under the ministry of an insignificant, self-appointed prophet named John. Things would be different in the universe after this event, according to Mark.

What happens next defends Mark's position. The ancient Rabbis taught that when God speaks, "the daughter of his voice," or "the echo of his voice," is heard. But Mark does not record God's voice in that way. Instead, Mark says that the very voice of Jesus' heavenly Father spoke words of approval over his Son. "You are my dearly loved Son, and you bring me great joy" (Mark 1:11). John's baptism of Jesus serves as a declaration to the world across time that Jesus was and is the Son of God.

Now remember that all three Gospels agree: as John baptized Jesus, the Holy Spirit, like a dove, settled on Jesus and the voice of his Father was heard. I call this scene "the Trinity's family portrait," as it is one of the rare times in the Bible where all three Persons of the Trinity appear in the same scene. The Father said of the Holy Spirit–blanketed Son, "You are my dearly loved Son, and you bring me great joy." In the South, the Father would have said, "That's my boy!" Jesus' baptism was his ordination service. Secured in his identity as the beloved son of Abba Father, Jesus began his ministry.

I want you to notice that Jesus' status as the beloved of the Father is not based on performance. Jesus hadn't done a thing to "earn" this declaration. His Father gave it to him. He had not yet taught a single lesson, preached a single sermon, or healed a single person. The lesson here for us is simple. Our "being" (who we are in relationship to God) goes before or precedes our "doing" (what we do for God). My identity in God (who I am) goes before my activity for God (what I do). My roots (identity) come before my wings (mission). This is the upside-down way of the Kingdom of God. In our culture, we are performance obsessed. We like winners and superstars. But Jesus' Kingdom flips everything on its head.

In my office at the church, I have the following quotation hanging on my wall, 4 foot by 3 foot wide. It has become a sort of life mantra for me. I made it so large because I tend to forget this simple yet profound message about my *being* going before my *doing*. It's a quote from Brennan Manning's book *All Is Grace*. This ragamuffin follower of Jesus penned this weighty reminder for hard-headed, performance-addicted people like me:

> My life is a witness to vulgar grace—a grace that amazes as it offends. A grace that pays the eager beaver who works all day long the same wages as the grinning drunk who shows up at ten til five. A grace that hikes up the robe and runs breakneck toward the prodigal reeking of sin and wraps him

up and decides to throw a party no ifs, ands, or buts. A grace that raises bloodshot eyes to a dying thief's request—"Please, remember me"—and assures him, "You bet!" A grace that is the pleasure of the Father, fleshed out in the carpenter Messiah, Jesus the Christ, who left His Father's side not for heaven's sake but for our sakes, yours and mine. This vulgar grace is indiscriminate compassion. It works without asking anything of us. It's not cheap. It's free, and as such will always be a banana peel for the orthodox foot and a fairy tale for the grown-up sensibility. Grace is sufficient even though we huff and puff with all our might to try to find something or someone it cannot cover. Grace is enough. He is enough. Jesus is enough.[28]

Jesus' baptism affirms this overwhelming truth about God's messy grace and our identity.

When Temptation Knocks at My Door

Three of the four biblical narratives of Jesus' life identically record that Jesus was baptized and then he was tempted by the devil in the wilderness. Luke tells it this way:

Then Jesus, full of the Holy Spirit, returned from the Jordan River. He was led by the Spirit in the wilderness, where he was tempted by the devil for forty days. Jesus ate nothing all that time and became very hungry. Then the devil said to him, "If you are the Son of God, tell this stone to become a loaf of bread." But Jesus told him, "No! The Scriptures say, 'People do not live by bread alone.'" Then the devil took him up and revealed to him all the kingdoms of the world in a moment of time. "I will give you the glory of these kingdoms and authority over them," the devil said, "because they are mine to give to anyone I please. I will give it all to you if you will worship me." Jesus replied, "The Scriptures

---

28.   Brennan Manning, *All Is Grace: A Ragamuffin Memoir* (Colorado Springs: David C. Cook, 2015), 194.

say, 'You must worship the Lord your God and serve only him.'" Then the devil took him to Jerusalem, to the highest point of the Temple, and said, "If you are the Son of God, jump off! For the Scriptures say, 'He will order his angels to protect and guard you. And they will hold you up with their hands so you won't even hurt your foot on a stone.'" Jesus responded, "The Scriptures also say, 'You must not test the Lord your God.'" When the devil had finished tempting Jesus, he left him until the next opportunity came. (Luke 4:1-13 NLT)

We see in the sequence of these two experiences of Jesus (first his baptism then his temptation in the wilderness by the devil) a real and helpful pattern for those of us who follow Jesus. We are often most vulnerable to what Paul calls "the fiery arrows of the devil" (Ephesians 6:16) right after our mountaintop encounters with God. The devil is wily and shrewd. After you've heard the welcoming words of the Father, have been immersed in the waters of Jesus' love, or have felt the winds of the Holy Spirit blowing on you, Satan, the one Peter calls a prowling, roaring lion (1 Peter 5:8), knows when to pounce. I've seen many a Christian fall to the evil one's tricks after record-breaking, life-transforming events in which God personally used them mightily. I've experienced the same myself. Did you know that anxiety, second-guessing, and depression sneak up on preachers on Sunday night and Monday morning after preaching? Do I have stories! Temptation to all kinds of unhealthy and unholy behavior and beliefs from the devil often creep in after great God victories in our lives.

Luke's retelling of the story offers us three important insights for our journey into the cave of temptation. First, Luke says, "Then Jesus, full of the Holy Spirit, returned from the Jordan River" (Luke 4:1a NLT). Here's another simple yet profound truth. If you're going to be tempted by the devil, you'd better be full of the Holy Spirit! Fresh off his Daddy's public approval, Jesus was overflowing in the

Spirit's presence and power. He came into this forty-day season with his spiritual armor on. Two decades later, Paul would write the words of caution to the missionary outposts of Jesus meeting in homes these words: "A final word: Be strong in the Lord and in his mighty power. Put on all of God's armor so that you will be able to stand firm against all strategies of the devil" (Ephesians 6:10-11 NLT).

One of the realities of my forty-five-year pilgrimage with Jesus is that Holy Spirit leaks out of me. Take for example, when I'm driving down Highway 41 in Fort Myers, Florida, and all my friends from up north are visiting us during that time of the year we call "Season." They have the audacity to drive the speed limit in the fast lane when I'm running late for a meeting to do the work of God, and sometimes in my frustration the Spirit leaks out, and then words come out of my mouth that a follower of Jesus ought not say. Am I alone? God wants to help Holy Spirit–leaking Christ followers like us.

I love the translation of Ephesians 5:18 from The Amplified Bible. "Do not get drunk with wine, for that is wickedness (corruption, stupidity), but be filled with the [Holy] Spirit and constantly guided by Him (Ephesians 5:18 AMP).I think it's awesome that the translators put the word "stupidity" in there. It's like Paul is saying to us that there are two kinds of spirits, the spirits of wine and the Holy Spirit. We can choose to be drunk or intoxicated with either. To those being intoxicated with wine, he'd say, "That's stupid." Instead, Paul invites apprentices of Jesus who leak the Holy Spirit to "be filled with the Holy Spirit and constantly guided by Him."

So, how do I get filled with Holy Spirit? For much of my early Christian life, I thought that people "filled with the Holy Spirit" were like people with spiritual PhDs, that being led by the Holy Spirit was for the elite disciples, the top 1 percent, the VIP disciples of Jesus. Nothing could be further from the truth. The Bible paints a different picture. Being filled with the Holy Spirit is not for heroes of the faith, but regular, ordinary, and in fact, "broken" and weak people who have entrusted their lives to Jesus, sometimes just out of sheer desperation. Author Mike Pilavachi, in his book *Everyday Supernatural*, writes: "The weaker we are, the more we lean on God for strength. The more broken we are, the more cracks there are for the Spirit to pour out through. The history of the church has never been about great men and women of God, it's always been about the great God of men and women."[29] Being filled with the Holy Spirit is not about our strength but God's strength. We simply need to be available, aware, and alert to what God wants to do in us and through us.

Jesus taught us how to get filled with the Holy Spirit. Notice he does not say you have to speak in tongues or do spiritual gymnastics. Listen to the words of our Rabbi:

> You fathers—if your children ask for a fish, do you give them a snake instead? Or if they ask for an egg, do you give them a scorpion? Of course not! So if you sinful people know how to give good gifts to your children, how much more will your heavenly Father give the Holy Spirit to those who ask him. (Luke 11:11-13)

How do I get the Holy Spirit? I "ask" for the Holy Spirit, and my Father, my Abba, my Daddy in heaven who loves to give generously will give me the Spirit. And when the Spirit leaks, I can keep asking to be filled again. I join the communion of saints who prayed for centuries, "Come, Holy Spirit, come." Jesus was filled with the Holy Spirit as he entered the cave of temptation.

Second, Luke records that *He was led by the Spirit in the wilderness* (Luke 4:1b). It's important to note that after hearing his Father's affirmation, the Holy Spirit led Jesus into a specific place, the wilderness. The Greek word for "wilderness" is *eremos*. It can be translated desert, deserted place, desolate place, solitary place, lonely place, or quiet place. It was a place filled with a multitude of caves. John Mark

---

29. Mike Pilavachi and Andy Croft, *Everyday Supernatural* (Colorado Springs: David C. Cook, 2016), 67.

Comer in his masterful book *The Ruthless Elimination of Hurry* says that for years he thought of the desert as a place of weakness but realized he had it backwards. [30] The desert was not a place of weakness for Jesus but rather a place of strength. His *eremos* place was where Jesus went to get reconnected with his Father. And remember that the text is clear. The *Spirit* led Jesus into the wilderness. Jesus' intent in heading into the wilderness for forty days was to be with his Father in a solitary place of prayer and fasting. In this sacred space he would also be tempted. Caves in these days were used as tombs for burying dead people. Jesus would be placed in a cave at the end of his life, but you could argue that this earlier cave, the cave of temptation, was just as "life or death" for Jesus. If he stumbled here at the beginning of his earthly ministry, the redemptive purposes of his mission could be thwarted. Victory in this cave of temptation in the wilderness would point to victory in the Garden Tomb in Jerusalem.

We see over and over again in all four of the Gospels that Jesus went to an *eremos* place, a deserted, desolate, solitary place to be with his Father. Thirty-two times, the word *eremos* is found in the Gospels, and most of the times it is used specifically to describe Jesus going into the wilderness to pray. Let me ask you. Do you have an *eremos* place? Do you have a lonely place for solitude, stillness, and silence? I asked a few of my colleagues at Grace Church to tell me where they went to be with the Father, and the places were amazingly diverse. Pastor Casey Culbreth told me that her *eremos* place is a park on the riverbanks of the Caloosahatchee River. Pastor Wes Olds told me that his quiet place is his back patio that looks out over a nature preserve. Pastor Taylor Brown said that his deserted place was a coffee shop with headphones on listening to worship music. For me, it's my study at home. Do you have a set aside place to be with God? Jesus went into the wilderness to be with God. Jesus entered this

30. John Mark Comer, *The Ruthless Elimination of Hurry* (Colorado Springs: Water-Brook, 2019), 124–25.

cave to be with his Father. It was a place of intimacy, a womb-like environment to be nurtured by God.

Third, Luke records that as the Spirit led Jesus into the wilderness, there "he was tempted by the devil for forty days. Jesus ate nothing all that time and became very hungry" (Luke 4:2 NLT). For years I thought that Jesus did not eat or drink anything for forty days and then, on "day forty," He was tempted; but that's not what the Bible teaches. Luke is careful to say that the temptation of Jesus lasted for forty days! That takes the intensity of Jesus' temptation up a bunch! This journey was intense and prolonged for him.

Jesus' half-brother, James, describes the lingering and ever-increasing dynamic of temptation when he writes, "Temptation comes from our own desires, which entice us and drag us away. These desires give birth to sinful actions. And when sin is allowed to grow, it gives birth to death" (James 1:14-15 NLT). We tend to think of the "moment" of temptation when James reminds us that temptation lingers and grows in intensity and consequences. It's the warning wisdom of Ralph Waldo Emerson who wrote, "Sow a thought and you reap an action; sow an act and you reap a habit; sow a habit and you reap a character; sow a character and you reap a destiny."[31] This is the nature of temptation.

The Devil Made Me Do It?

I'm sure for some of you readers all this "devil" talk leaves you feeling uncomfortable. Folks of my generation can remember comedian Flip Wilson saying, "The devil made me do it." I have to agree that often we blame the devil for temptation toward things that may come from other sources. In my study of the Bible, I have made a discovery of what I call "the unholy trinity" of evil. Followers of Jesus confess in the Apostle's Creed belief in the triune God, Father,

---

31.   Attributed to Ralph Waldo Emerson.

Son, and Holy Spirit. My lingering in scripture for more than four decades has shown me that the Bible similarly describes evil in three ways: Satan and his demons, the world or culture, and our own inner selfish, sinful nature.

Satan is "evil above us." After encouraging Ephesian Christ followers to put on their spiritual armor, Paul describes our adversary this way. "For we are not fighting against flesh-and-blood enemies, but against evil rulers and authorities of the unseen world, against mighty powers in this dark world, and against evil spirits in the heavenly places" (Ephesians 6:12). From the opening pages of the Bible to the last, Satan and his horde of imps seek to undo the good work of God in people. C. S. Lewis, in his masterpiece *The Screwtape Letters*, gives us this cautionary word on giving the devil too much or too little attention:

> There are two equal and opposite errors into which our race can fall about the devils. One is to disbelieve in their existence. The other is to believe, and to feel an excessive and unhealthy interest in them. They themselves (the devils) are equally pleased by both errors and hail a materialist or a magician with the same delight.[32]

Second, in my reading of the Bible I have seen "evil around us." Often the phrase "the world" is used to describe the influence of the ungodly culture of followers of Jesus. The fourth Gospel writer, John, who called himself "the disciple whom Jesus loved" (talk about living secure in your identity as God's beloved) wrote in one of his three letters to the churches this caution.

> Do not love this world nor the things it offers you, for when you love the world, you do not have the love of the Father in you. For the world offers only a craving for physical pleasure, a craving for everything we see, and pride in our

32. C. S. Lewis, *The Screwtape Letters* (San Francisco: HarperSanFrancisco, 2001), ix.

achievements and possessions. These are not from the Father but are from this world. And this world is fading away, along with everything that people crave. But anyone who does what pleases God will live forever. (1 John 2:15-17 NLT)

When John wrote this, he was not talking about not loving good food, great weather, and gracious friends. When he uses the phrase "do not love this world nor the things it offers you," he writes of the culture's endless thirst for things that destroy God's purposes for creation. All the -isms, from racism, sexism, ageism, and others, are attributed to the ways of the world. And we all know the lure to addictions, afflictions, and compulsive behaviors in our lives. We fight against this kind of stuff all the time.

Third, the Bible describes "evil inside us." This is our sinful nature. In trying to help the fledgling movement of Jesus in the region of Galatia, Paul taught them about the ongoing war between our deep selfish inner impulses and God. In his letter, he contrasts the fruit of the Spirit with the fruit of our sinful nature. He writes in Galatians 5:16-17 (NLT),

So I say, let the Holy Spirit guide your lives. Then you won't be doing what your sinful nature craves. The sinful nature wants to do evil, which is just the opposite of what the Spirit wants. And the Spirit gives us desires that are the opposite of what the sinful nature desires. These two forces are constantly fighting each other, so you are not free to carry out your good intentions.

Some translations use the word *flesh* here. Our flesh, our sinful nature, is in constant battle with the purposes of God in our lives. Years ago, our children were in a kids' musical at church that had an unforgettable song lyric. "I've got an 'I' problem. A 'me,' 'myself,' and 'I' problem." This is evil inside us.

So, here's what I believe about the source of temptation in our lives based on scripture as well as my personal experience and hearing about the experiences of countless others. I believe that all three forms of evil cooperate together to undo the grander and greater purposes of God in our lives. The devil and his demons, the world and its unholy enticements, and our own inner selfishness seek to destroy God's desires for wholeness and holiness in our lives. Like Jesus, we are in a fight for our lives!

Jesus Enters the Cave of Temptation

Full of the Spirit and with the intent of forty days of intimacy with his Father, Jesus entered the wilderness. His cave of intimacy would become a cave of temptation.

When my wife, Cheryl, and I were in Israel in the summer of 2013 during my sabbatical, we visited Jericho, the famed city whose walls fell in when Joshua and his army marched around it (Joshua 6). Many believe that it is in a cave in these mountains that surround Jericho where Jesus went and was tempted by the devil. This place is very desert-like, a real wilderness. Today there is a Greek Orthodox Monastery over the cave where they believe Jesus was tempted. Some of the caves that still exist in this mountain can be seen here. Jesus did some cave time here and his cave was the cave of temptation. Here the devil did not want to just "ding" Jesus. He wanted to destroy him. Baptized into his mission to rescue and redeem our broken, sin-filled, war-stained, bloody blue-green planet, the devil knew if he could trip Jesus up here, he could win the day.

So, what was the nature of the three temptations of the devil to trip up Jesus and thwart the grand redemptive purposes of God for the creation? Let me suggest that they were the same old types of temptations that the serpent gave Eve and Adam way back in Genesis 3. You see, the devil is sneaky but unoriginal. Jesus experienced three temptations. Each one challenged Jesus' understanding and experience of his Father's love as indicated in his baptism. They were full on, direct challenges to Jesus' relationship with the Father:

- His first invitation was the temptation to doubt the reliability of the Father's provision. Remember Jesus was on a forty-day fast. Nothing would have satisfied Jesus more than food and drink in that moment. Luke records the first lure this way. "Then the devil said to him, 'If you are the Son of God, tell this stone to become a loaf of bread'" (Luke 4:3). Woven into this temptation was the question, "Will God really provide for you your daily bread? Will God take care of you?"

- Jesus' second temptation from the devil is the temptation to doubt the legitimacy of the Father's praiseworthiness. The devil was writing checks he could not cash when he said to Jesus, "I will give you the glory of these kingdoms and authority over them . . . because they are mine to give to anyone I please. I will give it all to you if you will worship me" (Luke 4:6-7). He tempts Jesus with power that was not his to give so that Jesus would worship the devil and not his Father.

- The third enticement was the temptation to doubt the dependability of the Father's protection. Luke 4:9-11 records, "Then the devil took him to Jerusalem, to the highest point of the Temple, and said, 'If you are the Son of God, jump off! For the Scriptures say, "He will order his angels to protect and guard you. And they will hold you up with their hands so you won't even hurt your foot on a stone."'" Would the Father really watch over him?

We see something more insidious than the temptation toward things like money, sex, and power at work here. Those would have been bad enough. Evil's lure came to destroy a deeper, more soulish need that Jesus had—to live securely and confidently as the Son of God. Jesus had just heard heaven's clarion declaration, "You are my dearly loved Son, and you bring me great joy." In the wake of this confirmation, the devil threw all of the forces of evil against Jesus in order to challenge his identity as God's beloved.

Nothing has changed in 2000 years. The temptations that come into our lives every day have the potential to destroy us to the core. Moral failures like giving into sexual sin or financial greed are bad enough, but Jesus' atoning work on the cross can "wipe the slate clean." "What can wash away my sin? Nothing but the blood of Jesus." The devil wins the battle when we fail morally, but he wins the war when he demolishes our belovedness. This happens when we make that fatal mistake of believing that we didn't just fail, but that we are a failure. Evil wants to eradicate our identity as a child of God and person of worth. Henri J. M. Nouwen in his *Life of the Beloved* put it beautifully and accurately when he penned:

> Yes, there is that voice, the voice that speaks from above and from within and that whispers softly or declares loudly: "You are my Beloved, on you my favor rests." It certainly is not easy to hear that voice in a world filled with voices that shout: You are no good, you are ugly; you are worthless; you are despicable, you are nobody—unless you can demonstrate the opposite.[33]

The most dangerous part of entering the cave of temptation is the danger of identity destruction. We can exit it with false beliefs about our loving Father and the worth we have as his beloved children.

Winning in the Cave of Temptation

So, how can God and I win in the cave of temptation? Let me first remind you of this simple yet profound truth. Temptation is not sin. Temptation is the nudge to sin but it is not sin itself. I've met many a follower of Jesus who was racked with guilt and shame because he or she was tempted to sin. All that means is that he or she is alive and has a heartbeat! Paul helps us with this tough question

33. Henri J. M. Nouwen, *Life of the Beloved* (New York: Crossroad Publishing Company, 1992), 26.

about winning in the cave of temptation in two little verses found in 1 Corinthians 10:12-13: "If you think you are standing strong, be careful not to fall. The temptations in your life are no different from what others experience. And God is faithful. He will not allow the temptation to be more than you can stand. When you are tempted, he will show you a way out so that you can endure."

Paul gives us four insights here. First, I need to accept that my temptations are real. 1 Corinthians 10:12 (NLT) says, "If you think you are standing strong, be careful not to fall." Paul is writing to followers of Jesus here. He is reminding them that they "have feet of clay" (NLT). He recognizes the pattern that when they think they are invincible, they must be especially careful not to fall.

You've likely heard the phrase, "There but by the grace of God go I." A widely circulated story is that the English evangelical preacher and martyr, John Bradford, who lived from 1510–1555, is given credit for the phrase. He is said to have uttered this variant of the popular expression, "There but for the grace of God, goes John Bradford," when seeing criminals being led to the scaffold to be hung by the neck.

Wise is the Christ-follower who lives with this simple phrase resonating in his or her soul. "There but by the grace of God go I." Temptations are real and we are susceptible to them. Arrogance is the first step into the ditch. People ask me all the time why I self-identify as a Christ-follower in recovery from drugs and alcohol instead of saying, "I'm a Christ-follower who has been delivered from drugs and alcohol." The answer is easy. It's because when I forget where God found me, I'm likely to go back. Someone once told me, "Where God builds a sanctuary the devil builds a chapel." I learned in recovery that while I was in the rooms working on my recovery, my addiction was outside doing push-ups. Temptations are real.

The second way God wins us over in the cave of temptation is to recognize that our temptations are common. In 1 Corinthians

10:13a Paul writes, "The temptations in your life are no different from what others experience." This is the other side of the coin of the first insight. If point one reminds us that we are all vulnerable, point two reminds us that we are not terminally unique. Both are rooted in an unhealthy self-confidence.

Peter, a member of Jesus' executive team along with James and John, struggled with this unhealthy self-confidence. In the Upper Room at the Seder meal, Jesus told all the disciples that they would soon all fall away and abandon him. Peter's response was classic bravado: "Even if I must die with you, I will not deny you!" Matthew gives us the detail that "all the disciples said the same thing too" (Matthew 26:35 ESV). Peter and his colleagues forgot that the temptation was a common possibility for everyone. They did not have a case of terminal uniqueness simply because they had been walking with Jesus. Nor is there for us.

We are all vulnerable. Temptation is common to everyone. As mentioned, the basic types of temptation can be boiled down to money, sex, and power. As a follower of Jesus and a Christian pastor, all three raise their ugly head in my life daily. The enticement to have more and better stuff is a part of my daily battles. The lure to lust after women is very real. The pull toward puffing my chest up in power is strong in me. My vocation does not inoculate me from temptation. Evil doesn't care what my title is. No terminal uniqueness!

The third way to win in the cave of temptation is to realize that temptations are limited. 1 Corinthians 10:13b says, "And God is faithful. He will not allow the temptation to be more than you can stand" (NLT). Have you ever heard the saying, "God will never give you more than you can handle?" Not only is that not found in the Bible but it's a lie! My friends who wrestle with their addictions and compulsive behaviors are being given more than they can handle. My friends whose children are lost in unhealthy, unholy relationships to the point the parents want to "throw in the towel" are being given more than they can handle. The same thing is true of many who are struggling with the temptation to take shortcuts at work, with money, or at school, to name a few. Here's what the Bible teaches and it's true. God won't give you more than God can handle! Temptations are limited, but God is unlimited. God is faithful!

We need to have the right perspective about temptation. A boy was being bullied by some of the neighborhood kids. One night his father spotted the boy looking out the window with a telescope. Upon a closer look, the father noticed that the boy was looking out of the wrong side of the telescope. It made the objects he was looking at smaller rather than bigger. The father asked the son, "Son why are you looking out of the wrong end of the telescope?" To which the boy answered, "I'm looking at the bullies across the street, and I wanted them to look smaller than they really are!" You see, God is faithful. We have a bully. His name is the devil, but he is smaller than he appears with our faithful God on our side. Remember, temptations are limited!

Finally, when I'm in the cave of temptation, I can win when I believe my temptations can be overcome. Paul finishes 1 Corinthians 10:13c with these words of encouragement. "When you are tempted, he will show you a way out so that you can endure" (NLT). A way out! The promise of God is that God is a faithful God and will show you a way out. But remember, it's God who will show the way. Let me share with you God's ways of escape for the temptation to money, sex, and power in my life.

- My wife Cheryl and I have gotten out of debt, and we have made a budget that we live by. Staying out of debt is a constant battle, but our budget is God's way of escape for money temptations for us.

- God's way of escape for sexual temptation for me includes the support of my two best friends, Dale and Matthew. Not only in my day-to-day existence here in Southwest Florida but when I travel to speak, I arrange for my two best buddies to check my holiness of heart and life. They explicitly ask me, "Jorge what are you watching on your TV and computer?" These guys are God's way of escape for me.

- Every other week, I have a face-to-face accountability meeting with my coach, Craig, to talk about my relationship with God and the condition of my ministry. Craig regularly pushes into my propensity to "lord it over" people. This relationship is God's way of escape from power temptation for me.

God always provides a way out. Whether it's money, sex, or power, there is a way out. The real question is are we looking for it? Remember temptation is real, common, limited, and can be overcome.

Let me remind you of one more thing. Remember that the Bible teaches that Jesus was mysteriously 100 percent God and 100 percent human being. If anything screams to be heard in the temptation of Jesus it is his humanity. Hebrews 4:14-16 (NIV) affirms this as well:

> Therefore, since we have a great high priest who has ascended into heaven, Jesus the Son of God, let us hold firmly to the faith we profess. For we do not have a high priest who is unable to empathize with our weaknesses, but we have one who has been tempted in every way, just as we are—yet he did not sin. Let us then approach God's throne of grace with confidence, so that we may receive mercy and find grace to help us in our time of need.

Notice the phrase "but we have one who has been tempted in every way, just as we are—yet he did not sin." Does it say Jesus was tempted in "some of the ways" we are tempted? No! It says in "every way." Here's what I want to remind you to do when evil in all its insidious forms raises its ugly tempting head for money or sex or power or anything else in your life. You have a Savior who knows your pain, and he died on the cross and rose from the dead so that you can have victory over the cave of temptation.

Notice the last line: "Let us then approach God's throne of grace with confidence, so that we may receive mercy and find grace to help us in our time of need." When we are tempted to sin because of Jesus, we are invited to confidently and boldly approach the throne of grace because Jesus has gone before us. We can find in God the mercy and grace we need to endure the temptation. We have a savior who empathizes with us in the fight with temptation.

I Will Fight for You

Now each time Jesus faced one of these temptations of pleasure or position or possessions, Jesus responded with "For the scriptures say"; some translations put it "It is written." Jesus is referring to more than just a Bible verse in the Old Testament. Jesus is referring to the Author of the scriptures. He's referring to his good, good Father, the One who is well pleased with Jesus, the One who called Jesus his beloved, the One who is pleased with Him regardless of his performance. Jesus was declaring what the Bible says over and over again: "My God will fight for me!"

In the height of our son's struggle with addictions, I found myself speaking at an event for a mission sending organization. Here's the irony again. My public life was soaring. Grace Church was capturing the attention of church leaders, and my invite list to speak blew up. Book writing opportunities and awards from the denomination and my seminary came. Publicly, it all looked great. That's why I was invited to speak. But back home, our son was slowly dying in his addiction, and as his parents, we were slowly dying too. Our temptation was to "throw in the towel," and it came regularly. "Give up," "give in" seemed like a solution in our darkest hours.

The worship leader at the event was the number one worship leader in Brazil. He is the "Chris Tomlin" of Brazil. He stood up one night and said, "I don't know who this song is for, but I believe the Holy Spirit wants to help someone who is ready to give up." Then he began to sing this amazing song with the simple chorus of God saying to us, "I will fight for you." Tears of surrender drowned the fiery darts of the devil that night. The whisper of the Holy Spirit drowned out the voice of the accuser. The promise of God undermined the indictments of Satan. God would fight for our boy. Temptation was pushed back that night with a simple, "It is written!" King Jesus fights for us! So, no matter what temptation you are fighting today, whether money, sex, power, or anything else, you can be victor and not victim because Jesus has won the victory for you!

The unknown and unnamed writer of the book of Hebrews was trying to encourage first century followers of Jesus who were tempted to abandon their faith. The temptation was real, as the Romans were persecuting them ruthlessly. In this amazing New Testament letter, the author declares "Don't give up!" over and over again. In Hebrews 4, the author calls Jesus their "High Priest." This would have been a powerful metaphor to the readers because the High Priest was the most important religious leader of their faith. Traced back to Aaron, the brother of Moses, in the Levite tribe, the High Priest oversaw the sacrificial system at the Temple in Jerusalem and performed the ritual for their most holy day, the Day of Atonement on behalf of all of Israel (Leviticus 16).

When we are in the cave of temptation, we can draw strength from knowing that Jesus was there too. Tempted in every way like us, Jesus "gets" the tug of evil. This emboldens us to come to God's gracious presence even when we succumb to evil's temptations. In the presence of Jesus, our High Priest, he extends both grace (getting what we don't deserve) and mercy (not getting what we do deserve).

Chapter Five: With Mary and Martha in the Cave of Grief

You have to walk through the valley of the shadow of death.
You don't have to camp out there.

—Wes Olds

Give sorrow words: the grief that does not speak
Whispers the o'er-fraught heart and bids it break.

—William Shakespeare, Macbeth, Act 4, Scene 3

All of this "cave" talk got me wondering, "How many caves are there in Israel?" Quick research on the web helped me to discover that experts in earth sciences have gathered a census of the number of caves in the Holy Land. On the Israel21c website, I learned:

> "It's nearly impossible to count Israel's caves because new ones are discovered every day," says Prof. Amos Frumkin, director of the Cave Research Unit at the Hebrew University of Jerusalem's geography department. "Right now we have about 1,200 registered caves in our database, but I can estimate roughly that there are many thousands," he tells ISRAEL21c. "Most of the caves are formed by rainwater infiltrating underground and dissolving the soluble rock that

is plentiful in Israel. Others were created by people carving out spaces for quarries, living quarters, industry, burial, hiding or other reasons," says Frumkin.[34]

1200-plus caves! That sounds like a lot of places to run and hide or run and heal, both then and now!

One insight by Professor Frumkin really got me pondering. He noted that most caves are formed naturally while others are formed by people, for "burial, hiding, or other reasons." People can create their own caves, and sometimes we dig and crawl into these caves just to survive. The wife who is daily brutalized with weaponized words and detonated fists builds a cave of survival to hide from and endure the beatings. She turns to alcohol to cope with her suffering. It's sadly understandable. This is her cave of survival. The innocent boy who grows up in a home filled with addictions and the accompanying parental narcissism and neglect digs a cave to escape and manage the family of origin dysfunction. He obsessively loses himself in the world of video games to get away from the misery. It's woefully reasonable. This is his cavern of safety. Who can blame the fearful wife or the frightened little boy?

Mental health professionals call these "coping mechanisms." The American Psychological Association Dictionary defines a *coping mechanism* as "any conscious or nonconscious adjustment or adaptation that decreases tension and anxiety in a stressful experience or situation. Modifying maladaptive coping mechanisms is often the focus of psychological interventions." Clearly, the abused wife's alcoholism and the neglected boy's cyber-addiction are understandable, yet sadly also "maladaptive coping mechanisms." They are often caves of suffering from which the awful possibility of lifelong living occurs. The lure to set up one's life in these handmade caverns of

34.   Abigail Klein Leichman et al., "Escape the Heat in Israel's Top 10 Caves," IS-RAEL21c, August 5, 2015, https://www.israel21c.org/top-10-caves-of-israel/.

survival is strong for all of us as we manage the pains and sorrows of living. Sometimes we dig our own caves.

Dark Valleys and Deep Caves

Another powerful geographical metaphor is the valley. We often compare mountaintop "highs" with deep valley "lows." Yet, in the Bible the use of "valleys" is more diverse. They can be good places of abundance (Deuteronomy 8:7; 11:11) and fertility (Numbers 13:23-24; Psalm 65:13) as well. Also, battle lines were frequently drawn in valleys in the pages of scripture (Genesis 14:1-16). But sadly, the valley was often a very real place of idolatry for God's people, which the prophets of God like Jeremiah would judge with strong indictments, such as, "You say, 'That's not true! I haven't worshiped the images of Baal!' But how can you say that? Go and look in any valley in the land! Face the awful sins you have done. You are like a restless female camel desperately searching for a mate" (Jeremiah 2:23). Used figuratively, valleys in the Bible were most often places of sadness and sorrow. Maybe you're already thinking about one use in the famous shepherd's psalm, Psalm 23.

One of my mentors, Howard Olds, like all celebrated orators, had great one-liners. One of his most memorable was, "You gotta keep walkin'!" I can still hear Howard getting his preach on with his shouting voice. He had based this one-liner on the famous lyric from the shepherd-warrior King and poet, David, who reminds us in Psalm 23:4, "Even when I walk through the darkest valley, I will not be afraid, for you are close beside me. Your rod and your staff protect and comfort me." David was clear. We "walk through the darkest valley." It is the place Eugene Peterson masterfully called "Death Valley" in his translation of Psalm 23:4. But Howard is right. We really don't have to set up our home in Death Valley. God's promise is to be our Companion as we walk through the darkest moments of life. "You gotta keep walkin'!"

No wonder decades later, sitting on the front row of Grace Church, Cape Coral campus, I almost jumped out of my skin when Howard's son, who is my spiritual son, was preaching on Psalm 23 and said, "You have to walk through the valley of the shadow of death. You don't have to camp out there." Like father, like son. The acorn doesn't fall too far from the tree. Father and son know what the Bible says. "You gotta keep walkin'!" Or as the quote of unknown origins says, "Pain is inevitable. Suffering is optional." The dark valley may be a place of coping for a while, but we can move on and even grow in this sorrowful gorge. It can be a place we stop and visit on life's journey, but it does not have to be our permanent destination.

So, let's move from the dark valley biblical metaphor back to the dark cave. And let's be honest. No cave has the intense draw to "setting up camp" and making it a permanent destination more than the cave of grief. I think we'd all agree that in the cave of grief, we experience a deep level of pain and suffering unlike no other.

Grief Defined

What is grief? Let's go back to the American Psychological Association Dictionary for their definition:

> [Grief is] the anguish experienced after significant loss, usually the death of a beloved person. . . . Grief often includes physiological distress, separation anxiety, confusion, yearning, obsessive dwelling on the past, and apprehension about the future. Intense grief can become life-threatening through disruption of the immune system, self-neglect, and suicidal thoughts. Grief may also take the form of regret for something lost, remorse for something done, or sorrow for a mishap to oneself.

Clinically, this sounds and feels right to me. But their definition is a bit mechanical. Grief gets into your bones. It lives beneath the surface. We need a definition of grief that is more organic, more human on our journey in and through the cave of grief.

The greatest tragedy of the great Christian thinker C. S. Lewis' life seemed to be the loss of his wife, Joy Davidman, who died of cancer in 1960. Her death tested his faith like very little had. C. S. Lewis famously wrote of his journey through the valley of the shadow of death in his classic little book, "A Grief Observed." In it he described grief this way:

> No one ever told me that grief felt so like fear. I am not afraid, but the sensation is like being afraid. The same fluttering in the stomach, the same restlessness, the yawning. I keep on swallowing.
>
> At other times it feels like being mildly drunk, or concussed. There is a sort of invisible blanket between the world and me. I find it hard to take in what anyone says. Or perhaps, hard to want to take it in. It is so uninteresting. Yet I want the others to be about me. I dread the moments when the house is empty. If only they would talk to one another and not to me.[35]

Lewis got even more graphic when he compares the death of a loved one to an amputation. Yes, grief feels "like fear," "like being mildly drunk or concussed," like "an amputation." These more accurately describe the journey into the cave of grief. Whether it's the loss of a loved one through death or the loss of a life dream that has been dashed against the cruel rocks of circumstance, grief is an unwelcomed intruder that leaves the best of us reeling.

My pastoral colleague in Florida, Dr. Samuel Wright, wrote of his journey of grief in his book *Heartbreak to Hope*. His son, Samuel Jr., died in a motorcycle accident in California at the age of thirty-two. This sent Samuel Sr., his wife Yvonne, sister Rebekah, and all

---

35.　C.S. Lewis, *A Grief Observed* (New York: HarperCollins Publishers, 1994), 19.

those who loved Samuel Jr. deep into the cave of grief. With a shepherd's heart and a scholar's mind, Samuel Sr. invites his readers to learn to grieve in his book. He bravely titles chapter 1 and a poem he wrote at the ten-month mark of Samuel's death, "Abused by Grief."[36]

> It has been ten months since
> Our son Samuel was killed.
>
> In the beginning the
> Monstrous gorilla
> Pounced on me
> Beating my chest
> With one massive fist,
> Smothering
> My face with his other
> Without a moment's relief.
>
> The towering brute
> Shook me like a rag doll
> Dragged me by the hair
> From one side of the cage
> To the other;
> Tossed me around
> Stomped me down
> Picked me up by the throat
> Squeezed the life out of me.
>
> This teething giant
> Chomped on me like a human chew toy.
> My face pressed against
> The bars as he pounded my back.
> No escape from his fury

---

36. Samuel L. Wright, Sr., *Heartbreak to Hope* (Orlando, FL: EA Books Publishing, 2016), 9–11.

No strength to endure
No hope.

I could not breath.
I could not rest.
I could not fight back.
I could not sleep.
I could not heal.
Locked in the cage
With this massive foe.

We sit in the cage together
Now that I'm able to sit up
Still with considerable pain.
My wounds have scabbed over
He raises his fist and I flinch
In the corner.
His yellow eyes smile.
His glare terrifies me
In total submission
Which satisfies Grief
Most of the time.

But like Samson
My hair is growing back
I have regained some strength
I managed to stand,
Which resulted in a severe beating.
Grief suffers no competition.

Lying on my back
Through bloodied eyes
I notice
This cage has no roof!

Escape might be possible.
But the bars are too high
I am too weak
To shinny up them.

I measure the enormous
Primate whose back is toward me.
He is leaning forward looking out the bars
Staring in to the darkness.
His massive furry skull
Nearly reaches the top.

Could I use Grief
Like a ramp
To climb out of
This torture chamber?
I have to be quick.
No room for a running start.
I have to try.

Samuel Sr. courageously reminds us of the long and painful journey in the cave of grief. No two people experience the same journey even though they may share the same name like "death," or "divorce," or "bankruptcy." But there is a commonness too. Anyone who has entered the cave of grief knows the weight of the monstrous gorilla.

Dr. Terry Wardle in an episode of the "Church Pulse Weekly" podcast spoke during the height of the Covid pandemic to the issue of grief and aimed his comments specifically at pastors and their unique challenges of leading through an epidemic. [37] Much of what

37. Carey Nieuwhof and David Kinnaman, "ChurchPulse Weekly: 062: Dr. Terry Wardle on the Damage of Unresolved Wounds and the Risk and Gifts of Vulnerability on Apple Podcasts," Apple Podcasts, May 26, 2021, https://podcasts.apple.com/us/podcast/062-dr-terry-wardle-on-damage-unresolved-wounds-risk/id1503586969?i=1000523234947.

he spoke about appeals to common humanity regardless of vocation and calling. He used the phrase "ungrieved losses" to describe grief. Then he said, "Every loss in life demands an appropriate season of grieving whether your loss is your favorite person or your favorite pen." Every loss? Yes, he said "every loss." This cave of grief is tricky because it involves "every loss," the loss of a dearly loved person, a deeply held dream, a profoundly meaningful relationship, or a severely loved job.

With Two Sisters in the Cave of Grief

So, with this understanding of grief, let's go with two sisters, Mary and Martha, into their cave of grief. One of the things we as Bible readers often unconsciously do is comingle stories from the four Gospel narratives of Jesus' life and ministry into one story. It's so easy to do. The Gospel of Mark and the Gospel of Luke may tell a very similar story while the Gospel of Matthew tells a slightly different version of the same story, and the Gospel of John leaves the story out altogether. We recall the story as "one big story" forgetting that each narrative of Jesus' life was written by a unique author with a specific goal in mind. For example, The Gospel of Mark tells the reader from the first words that it was clearly written with goal of convincing readers, "This is the Good News about Jesus the Messiah, the Son of God" (Mark 1:1). While the Gospel of John waits to the end of the narrative to tell us his aim. "The disciples saw Jesus do many other miraculous signs in addition to the ones recorded in this book. But these are written so that you may continue to believe that Jesus is the Messiah, the Son of God, and that by believing in him you will have life by the power of his name" (John 20:30-31). The careful student of God's Word who "correctly explains the word of truth" (2 Timothy 2:15) and desires to be, in the words of my seminary Professor Bob Mulholland, "shaped by the Word"[38] will keep this important Bible interpretation methodology in mind.

We are going to look at one of those stories that has all kinds of auxiliary stories found in other Gospel narratives that get comingled in. In the book of John, the fourth of the biographies of Jesus, we learn that Jesus had a relationship with a family of siblings made up of two sisters named Mary and Martha and their brother Lazarus. John tells us that Jesus loved all three of them (11:5). They lived in Bethany, a city on the Mount of Olives just a few miles from the city of Jerusalem.

Jesus on several occasions visited Bethany, but it's not clear that it was always at the home of these three (Matthew 21:17, 26:6; Mark 11:1, 11-12, 14:3; Luke 19:29, and 24:50). This is part of what I mean when I say we comingle Bible stories into one story. I've heard it said that these were Jesus' besties and that they hung out all the time. The biblical text does not seem to validate this. Jesus clearly went to the city where these three that he loved lived often, but perhaps not exclusively to their home.

In a later story in John's Gospel, John tells us another story about being in Bethany at the home of these three, deeply loved friends. The name "Bethany" literally means "village of the poor." Isn't it ironic that Jesus who came "to proclaim good news to the poor" (Matthew 4:18) loved being with these friends in the "village of the poor?"

> Six days before the Passover celebration began, Jesus arrived in Bethany, the home of Lazarus—the man he had raised from the dead. A dinner was prepared in Jesus' honor. Martha served, and Lazarus was among those who ate with him. Then Mary took a twelve-ounce jar of expensive perfume made from essence of nard, and she anointed Jesus' feet with it, wiping his feet with her hair. The house was filled with the fragrance. (John 12:1-3 NLT)

---

38. M. Robert Mulholland, *Shaped by the Word: The Power in Scripture in Spiritual Formation* (Nashville, TN: Upper Room, 1985)

This is a beautiful and tender story. Again, sometimes well-intentioned students of the Bible will comingle this story with the Matthew 26:6-13 story and the Mark 14:3-9 story of a woman who came to the house of Simon the Leper in the same village of Bethany and anointed Jesus' head with an alabaster flask of ointment of very costly pure nard. Same kind of anointing, different home and woman it seems. Sometimes the Luke 7:36-50 story of "a certain immoral woman from that (unnamed) city" (Luke 7:37) who interrupted Jesus' dinner at the home of Pharisee and anointed his feet with expensive oil and wiped them clean with her hair as she continually kissed them gets mixed in with the story of Mary, Martha, and Lazarus. Again, it's not clear from the text if this woman is Mary from John 12. Luke's Gospel does tell us another story about Jesus when the two sister's minus Lazarus get into a tussle about whether fixing a meal for Jesus or sitting at Jesus' feet was a more important thing to do (Luke 10:38-42). It's a fascinating story. Again, it's easy to see how we can merge all of these stories together.

With this clarification, let's go back to the story in John 11. The story begins with a crisis:

> A man named Lazarus was sick. He lived in Bethany with his sisters, Mary and Martha. This is the Mary who later poured the expensive perfume on the Lord's feet and wiped them with her hair. Her brother, Lazarus, was sick. So, the two sisters sent a message to Jesus telling him, "Lord, your dear friend is very sick" (John 11:1-3).

Mary and Martha were making their first painful steps in the direction of the cave of grief. Often these pilgrimages into dark caves are slow and tedious. Lazarus is receiving what the saints who do contemporary hospice ministry call palliative care. This is when tender loving professionals seek to relieve the pain of the dying without dealing with the cause of their lethal condition. It's helping the dying experience what we call God's "glorifying grace."

In desperation, these two loving sisters giving palliative care to their dying brother dial 9-1-1 for Jesus. They appeal to Jesus' *nearness* because of Lazarus' *dearness* to the Master. "Lord, your dear friend is very sick." The crisis of Lazarus' impending death required a geographical change in Jesus. Hearing the distant stories of Jesus' miraculous healing up north in the Galilee would not cut it for the two desperate women. They needed their own up-close-and-personal first-hand miracle. They need the gentler Healer in their house now. There was an urgency to their request.

John's commentary on this desperate situation takes an odd twist. Here's how John describes what happened when Jesus got word of his dearly loved friend's impending death:

> But when Jesus heard about it he said, "Lazarus's sickness will not end in death. No, it happened for the glory of God so that the Son of God will receive glory from this." So although Jesus loved Martha, Mary, and Lazarus, he stayed where he was for the next two days. (John 11:4-6)

This story is filled with comfort and trouble. It is comforting that Jesus says Lazarus' story isn't the end. It is comforting that God is going to be glorified. It is comforting that Jesus loves this family. But, let's go ahead and name the trouble with this verse. It's the "although." "So, although Jesus loved Martha, Mary, and Lazarus, he stayed where he was for the next two days." It's the elephant in the room and it is the disappointment of this family, and frankly countless families, who have walked through the valley of the shadow of death. Let's name it: How long does Jesus stay where he was? Two minutes? Two hours? No, he stays two days! I am glad to see the words of comfort in this story but I am troubled by the timing of Jesus. He still has a two-day journey ahead of him. That means from the perspective of his brokenhearted friends he's late to the scene! Have you ever felt that Jesus seems late?

Jesus' leadership here violates everything I have been taught as a leader and as a pastor over my entire life. I've been taught, "Never waste a crisis." I've learned to face problems. Tackle problems. Address problems. Don't lag. Don't delay. But Jesus in his counter-intuitive ways of the Kingdom waits. Now I can hear the more theologically astute thinking, "Yeah, but Jorge. He's God. He's got this." I concur, but Mary and Martha are not. They have limits, feet-of-clay like you and me. Let's just say it. Sometimes God's timing stinks. There. I said it. This was Mary and Martha's lived experience and if we are honest, at times, ours too.

N. T. Wright argues that Jesus wasn't playing with the suffering of Lazarus and his loved one here. He writes clarifying commentary of this waiting time of two days:

> What was Jesus doing? From the rest of the story, I think we can tell. He was praying. He was wrestling with the Father's will. The disciples were quite right (verse 8): the Judeans had been wanting to stone him, and surely he wouldn't think of going back just yet? Bethany was and is a small town just 2 miles or so from Jerusalem, on the eastern slopes of the Mount of Olives. Once you're there, you're within easy reach of the holy city. And who knows what would happen this time. . . . [H]e was praying for Lazarus, but he was also praying for wisdom and guidance as to his own plans and movements. Somehow the two were bound up together.[39]

I love how beautifully messy even Jesus' struggle to stay on mission is coupled with his own healthy and holy self-interest. It brings me some comfort to think that Jesus was in prayer and not cavalierly playing with the emotions of the desperate sisters caring for their dying loved one.

---

39. N. T. Wright, *John for Everyone*, vol. 2 (Louisville, KY: Westminster John Knox Press, 2004), 3.

You see, as the story continues, John tells us: "Finally, he said to his disciples, 'Let's go back to Judea.'" (John 11:7 NLT) The ragamuffins known in the Gospels as "the disciples" were full of compassion at Jesus' change in itinerary when they reminded their Rabbi that in their last visit to that region of Bethany and Jerusalem, the crowds tried to stone him to death. "Oh yeah, and Jesus if you haven't figured this out. People connect us. Your problems become our problems. Just filling you in Master." No, the Bible doesn't say that, but it can be inferred.

Jesus' response to the fearful disciples is classic and helpful especially for fearful disciples today. Look at Jesus' response to their safety concerns:

> Jesus replied, "There are twelve hours of daylight every day. During the day people can walk safely. They can see because they have the light of this world. But at night there is danger of stumbling because they have no light." (John 11:9-10)

This is a powerful metaphor. It's like Jesus is saying, "During the daytime, you can walk around carefree and without worry because you can see clearly, but at night you have to be careful so that you do not trip and fall. You need light." And what or better yet, who, is the light? It's Jesus himself. N. T. Wright comments again:

> He seems to have meant that the only way to know where you were going was to follow him. If you try to steer your course by your own understanding, you'll trip up, because you'll be in the dark. But if you stick close to him, and see the situation from his point of view, then, even if it means days and perhaps years of puzzlement, wondering why nothing seems to happen, you will come out at the right place in the end.[40]

40. Wright, *John for Everyone*, 4.

Jesus was not being cavalier or uncaring. He was once again pointing out the profound importance and simplicity of following Jesus even into the caves of potential suffering (for Jesus and the disciples) and the cave of grief (for the sisters).

Jesus then ends this prejourney briefing with the disciples by saying: "Our friend Lazarus has fallen asleep, but now I will go and wake him up" (John 11:11 NLT). It appears the disciples thought of "sleep" as literal sleep, while Jesus was speaking of "sleep" as death. John continues the dialogue with the disciples. "So he told them plainly, 'Lazarus is dead. And for your sakes, I'm glad I wasn't there, for now you will really believe. Come, let's go see him.'" (John 11:14-15). Jesus clarifies the current reality. Lazarus is not taking a nap. He's dead, but God is going to use Lazarus' death as a portal for trust in God. Thomas of "doubting Thomas fame" speaks up. "Let's go, too—and die with Jesus" (John 11:16b). This seems to be a sincere response on the part of the much-maligned apprentice of Jesus. And it was the right sincere response.

So off they go. John writes, "When Jesus arrived at Bethany, he was told that Lazarus had already been in his grave for four days" (John 11:17). This grave was literally a cave with a massive rock likely rolled in front of it. For Mary and Martha, it was their real cave of grief. Their beloved brother had died. Their grief over their personal loss was most likely compounded by the fact that Lazarus was most likely their provider and their link into the economy. His death would have meant disaster for Mary and Martha.

The four-day date stamp is significant. This was an important detail that John includes for us. In the first century, Jews believed that the soul hovered around the body for three days and then departed. In some of the tombs I have visited in Israel, I noticed there were even little openings for the soul to reenter or depart a body that was laid in a burial cave. What this detail means is that Lazarus was truly dead. There was no hope. His soul had already departed. This is nothing less than a cave of desperate grief.

With Jesus into the Cave of Grief

Now Jesus is face-to-face with the two sisters whom he loved and who are lost in the confusion of grief. Remember Samuel Wright's "monstrous gorilla?" He is standing on their chests. I love the raw honesty of Martha's loss described in John 11:20-22 as well as Mary's response in John 11:32 when Jesus arrives to their home:

> When Martha got word that Jesus was coming, she went to meet him. But Mary stayed in the house. Martha said to Jesus, "Lord, if only you had been here, my brother would not have died. But even now I know that God will give you whatever you ask." . . . When Mary arrived and saw Jesus, she fell at his feet and said, "Lord, if only you had been here, my brother would not have died."

Let's notice a couple of details that may help us in the cave of grief. First, notice that Mary and Martha each come to Jesus on their own timetables. Martha rushes out and meets Jesus on the road. Mary stays back for a bit. Isn't it interesting how these sisters give each other room to be on their own schedules? Grief demands we give each other the space we need to come to Jesus in our own time. No two sisters grieve at the same time and in the same way.

Second, notice that even though they come to Jesus at different times, they have the same statement: "Lord, if only you had been here, my brother would not have died." How many hours had they sat with Lazarus holding his hand, maybe wiping his sweat from his fever, holding onto hope that surely Jesus would show up? *Lord, if only you had been here!* How many times did they get up to look out the window with hopes of Jesus coming toward their house? How many silent prayers did they speak? "Hurry Lord." "Lord, if only you had been here." When Lazarus stopped breathing and Jesus was still not there, what disappointment must have gripped their soul. The shock must have felt like a kick in the gut, with anguish and disappointment that took their breath away. "Lord, if only you had been here!"

The confusion of grief causes us to search for answers and even interrogate God. But Jesus welcomes his friends just as they are, raw emotion and all. Jesus doesn't shame them or argue with them or condemn their struggle. Jesus doesn't enter into a debate about faith or tell them to "shape up." Jesus knows that the cave of grief is not a puzzle to be solved but a relationship to be lived. In the security of Jesus' embrace, they can live the questions.

I've found this in my life. I've discovered that Jesus is big enough and secure enough to handle my confusion, especially in times of grief. There is, after all, a whole book of the Bible called Lamentations. Do you know what lamentations actually means? It means "a passionate expression of grief and sorrow." Jesus is big enough to handle my confusion and my questions. Some of us may need to get a little more messy and honest in our prayers the way Mary and Martha did. "Lord, if only you had been here." Grief is not the time for sanitized Sunday school prayers. Grief demands we get real with Jesus.

One-third of the worship book in the center of our Bible called the book of Psalms is indeed laments. Yet, in every psalm of lament but one, the pattern is similar. The author dumps on God his or her sorrow in unbridled, uncensored honesty and then ends with doxology. There is something healthy and holy about Martha and Mary's "Lord, if only you had been here." Pent up emotions stuck and uncommunicated before God leads to all kinds of physical, emotional, spiritual, and relational dis-ease. Have you done this in your grief? Have you lifted your lament to the Lord or locked your lament down in your soul? Martha and Mary champion and model a better way.

Jesus Weeps with Me

The scene is surely chaotic. In this culture, at this time, there were actually professional mourners who often joined in to help a family grieve. What a career! Can you imagine being that parent at career day at school? "Now tell us what you do, Mr. Smith?" "Well, kids, I am a professional crier!" Talk about a downer. But John tells us that since Bethany was less than two miles away from Jerusalem, "many of the people had come to console Martha and Mary in their loss" (John 11:19). This no doubt included many of these professional mourners.

Mary comes out of the house and she falls at Jesus' feet, undoubtedly crying. John says Jesus looks around and sees all these others weeping, and something amazing happens: "Then Jesus wept" (John 11:35). My colleague Wes Olds loves to say, "Whenever a heart is broken, whenever a grave is opened, Jesus weeps." The Jesus who laughs and celebrates with us in good times of life on the mountaintops also laments and cries with us in the bad times of life in the valleys. Unlike the "Career-Criers" at the scene, Jesus weeps because he truly cares for Lazarus, Mary, and Martha. Being fully human, Jesus feels the depths of grief the same way we do.

It is not good to be alone and it is not good to weep alone. We need others to weep when we weep. An unseen and yet undeniable and unbreakable bond is created in the snot and saltiness of shared tears. As our son agonized with his addictions for nearly fifteen years, it was the shared tears of family and friends that helped us endure. There is a bond of friendship that is sealed in shared sorrows. Jesus weeps with his friends. He cries in company. He weeps with us when we weep, too. Jesus is our forever friend, and so he weeps with us in our dark and desperate cave of grief.

Over the decades while reading this story, I missed two small parts in verse 33 and verse 38:

When Jesus saw her weeping and saw the other people wailing with her, a deep anger welled up within him, and he was deeply troubled. (John 11:33 NLT)

…

Jesus was still angry as he arrived at the tomb. (John 11:38a NLT)

Why does Jesus weep? Jesus weeps because he is concerned. John says Jesus groans in spirit and is deeply troubled. The word groan in Greek is *embrimaomi,* which literally means "indignation, to snort with anger like a horse, to rebuke sternly, to be painfully moved." This gets accentuated in this story. Jesus was not just sad, but he was mad. He was groaning mad! The question begs to be asked "Why?" It's because he knows death is not God's good plan for us. Hear that again: Death is not a part of God's good plan for us. God is the author of life, not death. When a loved one dies, when wars won't cease, when children are abused, and disasters sweep over the innocent, Jesus weeps; his heart is touched with our grief.

St. Joseph's Old Cathedral sits directly across the street from the site of the 1995 Oklahoma City bombing when tragically 168 people were killed, including 19 children, and more than 500 were injured. Less than a year after that catastrophic day, the church erected a statue of Jesus weeping, simply called "And Jesus Wept." Jesus was and still is deeply troubled by what violence and death does to his good creation. It is no wonder that in the book of Isaiah Jesus is called "a man of sorrows, acquainted with deepest grief" (Isaiah 53:3b). Jesus heals us by crying with us in our caves of grief.

Life Touches Death

Jesus does not only listen and weep. He also takes action. Yes, Jesus is a *Wonderful Counselor* but he is also a *Mighty God.* (Isaiah

9:6) Death is no match for Jesus. Jesus makes his way to the hopeless grave of his dear friend Lazarus, now sealed for four days. John 11:39 gives us the commentary. "Roll the stone aside," Jesus told them. But Martha, the dead man's sister, protested, "Lord, he has been dead for four days. The smell will be terrible." The King James Version says it so well. "'Jesus said, Take ye away the stone.' Martha, the sister of him that was dead, saith unto him, 'Lord, by this time he stinketh.'" He stinketh! What seems now to be an utterly impossible stinky situation in human terms is transformed into a place of miraculous possibility in the presence of the Lord of life. Jesus grieves and Jesus weeps, but Jesus knows his Heavenly Father has power over death itself. Do you see the confidence Jesus has when he says, "Roll the stone aside"?

The same God who created the heavens and the earth with a word will raise Lazarus from the dead. Soon coagulated blood will begin to flow through Lazarus' arteries again. A stilled heart will begin to beat. Silent lungs will begin to breathe. Dark eyes with no sight will enliven again. Muscles stiff with rigor mortis loosen as starved cells receive oxygen again. Soon, Lazarus is a dead man walking.

I wanted so desperately to find his tombstone when I was in Israel because his would have had three dates on it: It would say something like "Born 5 AD. Died 29 AD (crossed out), Died again 75 AD." I've never seen a tombstone like that! I'll bet Lazarus was one of the most confident people in the world after walking out of that tomb. When the religious authorities threatened him to keep quiet about Jesus, I'm sure he said something like: "What are you gonna do? Kill me? I've been dead once!" Was Lazarus stressed when he got a cold? Probably not. Jesus' confidence became *his* confidence. Lazarus' name means "God helps" and I'm sure he was confident in God's help.

This miracle points not only to this moment where Lazarus gets a new lease on his old life and old body. This miracle points ahead to Jesus' soon-coming journey to the cross and tomb, and when he would be raised from the dead, victorious over death itself forever. We all know that eventually Lazarus would die. Jesus, with this miracle, is pointing his followers, then and now, to the finished work of Jesus on the cross and his resurrection we celebrate at Easter. Whenever Lazarus did die, his sisters could trust that they would be with their brother in eternity.

Death is not the end of the story. Whatever loss you and I are grieving right now is not the end of the story. When Jesus sees Lazarus' grave, he opens it. What we consider "dead ends" are only the beginning of eternal life. Jesus offers us that confidence today when we are standing in the gaping entrance to our own caves of grief. We can hear Jesus saying to us what he said to Martha *before* he raised Lazarus. "I am the resurrection and the life. Anyone who believes in me will live, even after dying. Everyone who lives in me and believes in me will never ever die. Do you believe this, Martha?" (John 11:25-26). He asked her to believe this while she was still deep in the cave of grief. And often Jesus asks this of us too.

This beautiful biblical story of Jesus and his three friends is a gift to us as we all inevitably will be beckoned to caves of grief in our lifetimes. In this cave we can encounter a Savior who empathetically weeps with us. But we can also encounter a Lord who defeats death. The words that Paul wrote decades later can embolden us in the cave of grief.

> And I am convinced that nothing can ever separate us from God's love. Neither death nor life, neither angels nor demons, neither our fears for today nor our worries about tomorrow—not even the powers of hell can separate us from God's love. No power in the sky above or in the earth below—indeed, nothing in all creation will ever be able to separate us from the love of God that is revealed in Christ Jesus our Lord (Romans 8:38-39).

This is our hope in the cave of grief!

Chapter Six: With Mary Magdalene in the Cave of Hopelessness

If there is life, there is hope.

—*Arlene Jackson*

As a young man, I'd hear grandparents say, "If I knew grandkids were this much fun, I would have skipped being a parent." Over the past fifteen years, I've adopted this mantra as my own. It began when my first grandchild, Mia was born. One of the greatest gifts of my life has been being "Drampa" (Mia could not get the "G" down) to Mia and her three siblings, Levi, Seth, and Zoe. Because they live a few miles away and are very active in our church, Cheryl and I have gotten to come alongside their parents and help raise them. Grand-parenting kids in our fifties and sixties has been so different than parenting our boys when we were in our twenties and thirties. I think I missed something in my first round of parenting and it's seeing the wide-eyed hopefulness of children.

Children see possibility all around them. Take for example how they play. Mia would transform into a princess as she played with her Disney Castle characters. As Levi drove an electric car we bought him, his robust imagination turned him into the movie character "Lightning McQueen." I can still hear him making motor noises as he drove his car with delight. The two youngest are still young children and they haven't lost much of this childlikeness. Seth still makes imaginative animals from his Legos, and Zoe can endlessly spin in circles singing gibberish with gleeful delight. Play flows naturally from a young, hopeful heart because life is full of possibility and potential.

As my grandkids have aged, I've also observed that the older two, now in their teens, have lost a lot of the childlike wonder and imagination. Brain research has taught us this can be chalked up to changes in the brain. Brain experts say that cognitive skills and rational thinking develop in a teen's brain into their early 20's. Sadly, it seems that for most young adults, an aging, rational brain works against this kind of childlike hopefulness. But it's not just brain chemistry that can rob our hopefulness. It's also the ordinary pains of life. In this chapter, we will journey with one of Jesus' apprentices, Mary Magdalene, into the cave of hopelessness. The itinerary for this pilgrimage to the cave begins seven long painful days before the first Easter, and I want to invite us to walk with Mary Magdalene and the other disciples to the abyss through the week we call "Holy Week." This seven-day, pain-filled journey sucked all the hope out of their lives but it led to an eighth day of hope.

A Grand Entrance?

Holy Week begins on the day we call "Palm Sunday," which we celebrate remembering Jesus as he entered Jerusalem riding a donkey, and he is welcomed by the masses like a conquering king on his chariot. All four of the Gospel narratives tell the story of Jesus' journey from Bethany to Jerusalem, the City of David.

Bethany was about two miles outside of Jerusalem. Now remember this is Passover time. Many of the pilgrims who travel to Jerusalem for this required festival would have traveled by foot to the place where God had promised to meet with his people, the Temple. If for example, you lived in Jericho, it's only about fifteen miles away, but here's the deal. Jericho is the lowest city on the planet at eight hundred feet below sea level, and Jerusalem sits at three thousand feet above sea level. The walk was arduous through hot, dry desert. So, you can imagine the delight worshippers had as they made their way to the top of the Mount of Olives and could not only see the first signs of vegetation but the beautiful city of David, Jerusalem.

Now imagine a huge family reunion with days of celebration, food, drink, and dancing. Family and friends from far away are gathering to remember the freedom that God brought his people, the Jews when he freed them from captivity in Egypt. The days of worship together are hopeful as they anticipate when, once again, they will be free, but this time not from Pharaoh and Egypt but Caesar and Rome. Much like their climb to Jerusalem, this climb to freedom would be arduous too. You can see why they so badly wanted a Messiah to free them from Rome's cruel grip. But they wanted a Messiah made in their own image.

On this first day of her seven-day journey, Mary Magdalene likely still had hope. Maybe the adoring crowd would love and follow Jesus like she did. Maybe there was possibility that this "Kingdom" of which Jesus spoke of could come "on earth as it is in heaven."

From the biblical narratives of the first Holy Week, we know nothing of what happened to Mary Magdalene from this Sunday parade to the awful events of what we call Good Friday. Likely later, she would hear about the final Seder meal Jesus had with his twelve apprentices, Judas' betrayal, Peter's denial, the religious leaders' venomous charges against her Master, Jesus' violent beating and his arduous journey carrying his own cross to Golgotha. But we do know from the Gospels that Mary Magdalene was an observer of the savagery her Master endured at the garbage heap on the outskirts of Jerusalem where Jesus hung between heaven and earth on the cross that Friday.

Hope Was Extinguished on Good Friday

By now it is about 9:00 in the morning on Friday and Jesus is heading to be crucified. If Roman scourging was barbaric, Roman crucifixion was equally savage and inhumane, maybe more so. Seneca, a Roman philosopher who lived in the first century, said that if you knew there was a likelihood of being arrested and crucified, it was better to commit suicide. Cicero, another first century Roman philosopher, called crucifixion the "cruelest and most disgusting punishment."

The Romans used crucifixion as a crime deterrent. Thus, they were performed in the public arenas. They wanted to make it crystal clear that if you crossed Roman law, you would be punished swiftly and severely. Now remember that Jesus has been flogged. His back has been laid open. Now he has to shoulder the hundred-pound cross beam and to make about a half-mile walk from the Praetorium to Golgotha where to be crucified.

There, Jesus was nailed to cross. Each of the four biographies tells of Jesus' crucifixion. Mark 15:25 simply states: "It was nine o'clock in the morning when they crucified [Jesus]." Hanging between heaven and earth, Jesus willingly gave his life on the cross. He hung from 9:00 in the morning until 3:00 in the afternoon. For six hours, the One who loved the outcast, the One who cared for women and children, the One who reached out to the diseased and the infirmed stretched out his arms in love for you and me! The hymn writer had it right when he wrote:

> When I survey the wondrous cross
> On which the Prince of glory died,
> My richest gain I count but loss,
> And pour contempt on all my pride.[41]

---

41. Isaac Watts, "When I Survey the Wondrous Cross," 1707.

Each of the four Gospel writers describes the moment of Jesus' death. Matthew and Mark tell us that Jesus shouted out and then died, but they do not recall the exact words Jesus shouted (Matthew 27:50, Mark 15:37). Luke gives us his recollection of the content of Jesus' shout when he pens, "Then Jesus shouted, "Father, I entrust my spirit into your hands!" And with those words he breathed his last" (Luke 23:46). John remembers it differently. "When Jesus had tasted it [the sour wine on a sponge], he said, "It is finished!" Then he bowed his head and gave up his spirit" (John 19:30 NLT). And with Jesus' death, Mary Magdalene's hope was extinguished.

Into the Cave of Hopelessness

Imagine what that first Passion Week felt like for those early followers of Jesus, the ones who had traveled with him around Galilee and Judea for months or even years? That last week sure started off with a bang—Jesus riding into town while people waved palm branches and sang to him, but things ended with a total bust. Their Master, their Rabbi, their Lord, went from "Conquering King" to "condemned criminal" in the span of less than a week. Imagine how high their hopes must have soared on Palm Sunday, only to be crushed into a million little pieces by Friday night.

No one would have felt this whiplash more than this woman from Galilee named Mary Magdalene, who had followed Jesus since the early days of his ministry. Many scholars believe that Mary Magdalene was one of the most faithful, most devoted of all of Jesus' followers. She's mentioned fourteen times in the Gospels, which is more than many of the twelve disciples. After Jesus was arrested on Thursday night and all of his (male) disciples fled and abandoned him, there was a small group of women who stayed near Jesus to the bitter end, even at the risk of being killed along with him. They loved him more than they loved their own lives. John tells us that as Jesus hung in agony on the cross, there were a few people that refused to let him suffer alone. "Standing near the cross were Jesus' mother, and his mother's sister, Mary (the wife of Clopas), and Mary Magdalene" (John 19:25 NLT). There was nowhere Mary Magdalene would have rather been than by the side of the man who had healed her and transformed her life. She never forgot who she used to be and where she had come from.

Luke introduces us to Mary Magdalene, way back in the early days of Jesus' ministry:

> Soon afterward Jesus began a tour of the nearby towns and villages, preaching and announcing the Good News about the kingdom of God. He took his twelve disciples with him along with some women who had been cured of evil spirits and diseases. Among them were Mary Magdalene, from whom he had cast out seven demons; Joanna, the wife of Chuza, Herod's business manager; Susanna; and many others who were contributing from their own resources to support Jesus and his disciples. (Luke 8:1–3 NLT)

Whatever was afflicting Mary, it must have been awful, because Luke describes it as "seven demons," meaning that it was complete, total, all-consuming pain and anguish for her mentally or physically, or both. She got her last name because she was from a city called "Magdala," on the shore of the Sea of Galilee. It was a place that was notorious as a haven for outlaws and prostitutes, and even though I don't think Mary was a prostitute, it probably didn't matter much, because she was a woman from the red light district of Galilee, the wrong side of town, unmarried, childless, and struggling with some kind of embarrassing affliction that probably subjected her to teasing and bullying throughout her childhood as well as isolation as an adult. She was the kind of person no one else wants or sees. Then one day, she met Jesus, and she was cured, healed, and transformed. Jesus saved her, and in response, she literally left everything behind and used all of her resources to support him and the disciples. She put all of her chips on the table. She was completely afflicted by seven demons all her life, but then she was completely devoted to the Lord who saved her. Her life in these days was full of hopeful possibility. She was experiencing what Paul would later call "new life" (Romans 6:4, Ephesians 4:22-24, 2 Corinthians 5:17).

From Mary Magdalene's perspective, everything was going great, especially on the week Jesus rode into town and everyone went crazy for him. Now, at last, people would see Jesus the way Mary did, as Savior and Healer. But somewhere along the way, things went off the rails. Five short days later, the same people turned on him, crazy with anger and demanding his death. Now she's standing at the city garbage dump, a few feet away from the crucified body of her Lord, holding his mom and watching rubberneckers mock him and spit at him, listening as he takes his last breaths.

Matthew picks up the story here:

> As evening approached, Joseph, a rich man from Arimathea who had become a follower of Jesus, went to Pilate and asked for Jesus' body. And Pilate issued an order to release it to him. Joseph took the body and wrapped it in a long sheet of clean linen cloth. He placed it in his own new tomb, which had been carved out of the rock. Then he rolled a great stone across the entrance and left. Both Mary Magdalene and the other Mary were sitting across from the tomb and watching. (Matthew 27:57-61 NLT)

At this point she's been awake for some 36 hours straight, but she doesn't care. She can't feel anything at this point anyway except for this ache, deep in her gut, this feeling that "it wasn't supposed to end like this." All of her hopes, her dreams, that she had treasured and pondered in her heart, that soared to even higher heights when Jesus rode into Jerusalem on a donkey and now her hopes have been crushed into a million little pieces. It wasn't supposed to end like this. This is the cave of hopelessness. And the Bible tells us that Mary

Magdalene was "sitting across from the tomb and watching." This is a hopeless situation. Possibility is gone.

What Is Hopelessness?

The doctor comes in and fingers through some official looking medical papers. He straightens his tie and clears his throat and somberly says to the haggard cancer patient, "It's hopeless. There is no more treatment. I'm sorry."

His wife fidgets with the meat and potato of her expensive meal at the swanky restaurant. All the hopes and fears of all the years bubble to the surface as she looks into the eyes of her husband of 18 years and says, "It's hopeless. I've tried. I just don't love you anymore."

The boss looked agitated all day. She was just not on her usual A-game. She seemed preoccupied. At the end of day, she called in her Assistant. "Listen, you know the company has been really struggling with our economy and we've crunched the numbers backwards and forward. It's hopeless. We've got to have major cutbacks or we will go bankrupt soon, I've got to let you go."

Each of these scenarios and countless others like them gets played out regularly in the drama that we call life. The names, dates, and the circumstances change, but the experience is common to us all. Add to the list the challenges of raising kids, starting businesses, going to school, buying a new home, or finding a new church, and you have the fodder of life. Sometimes sadly, these challenges end with "I'm sorry. It's hopeless."

What does it mean to be hopeless? To me to be hopeless means "I have no more options." No more treatment will fix it. No more counseling will resolve it. No more time will heal it. No more effort will change it. It's hope less. Hopelessness is the place where our prospects have been hijacked, and our dreams have been dashed. It's the place where the rug's been pulled out from under our future, where we're left scratching our heads wondering what in the world we should do next. It's the place where Mary Magdalene was on Friday night, and on Saturday, and on Sunday morning when she woke up.

Now, we know how this story ends. We know what God's about to do on Easter Sunday, but slow down. Don't run too quick. God wants to teach us in the cave of hopelessness with Mary. Maybe better yet, God wants to meet with us in the cave of hopelessness. Remember that Mary didn't know the end of the story. She was living it. This was the worst weekend of her life, and for all of Jesus' followers. Maybe you remember what the Cleopas and the unnamed disciples walking to Emmaus said to the resurrected Jesus whom they did not recognize. *We had hoped he was the Messiah who had come to rescue Israel* (Luke 24:21a). Mary, Cleopas and all the followers of Jesus had pinned all their aspirations for the future on Jesus.

The three days in the cave of hopelessness must have felt like three years to Mary. Pastor Jeff Manion calls this space, "the land between."[42] When the old is gone, but the new has not yet come, we're in the land between. "The land between" is Mary's cave of hopelessness. Maybe yours too. This is why her journey through the cave of hopelessness, through the "land between," can help us if we are in this cave or the next time we find ourselves there. Mary's story will show us that God meets us even in the cave of hopelessness. The tomb where Jesus was buried would soon become the turning point for the rest of Mary's life. And it all began when she found herself facing the same question that we do: What can I experience in the cave of hopelessness?

Mary's Experience in the Cave of Hopelessness

Like most experiences of life, the journey in the cave of hopelessness is an ever-expanding journey. I had little idea on the first day of

---

42.   Jeff Manion, *The Land Between: Finding God in Difficult Transitions* (Grand Rapids, MI: Zondervan, 2012).

my marriage or the first day of being a father or the first day of being a pastor what the experience would entail. It unfolded as I walked the trip. The joy and the learning was and is in the journey. The walk through all of these caves is a pilgrimage.

The first stage it seems to me for Mary and for us is that the cave of hopelessness can be a place of no understanding. John's narrative of Mary's experience that first Easter recounts it this way:

> Early on Sunday morning, while it was still dark, Mary Magdalene came to the tomb and found that the stone had been rolled away from the entrance. She ran and found Simon Peter and the other disciple, the one whom Jesus loved. She said, "They have taken the Lord's body out of the tomb, and we don't know where they have put him!" (John 20:1-2 NLT)

The ninth word in John 20 verse 1 is the word *dark*. It's one of the author's favorite metaphors. In his Gospel and three letters he regularly contrasts light and darkness. In his Gospel, he describes Jesus as "the light of the world" (John 8:12). In 1 John 1:5, he would pen: "This is the message we heard from Jesus and now declare to you: God is light, and there is no darkness in him at all." Look how John introduces us to Jesus at the beginning of chapter 1 in his beautiful cosmic poem about Jesus: "The Word gave life to everything that was created, and his life brought light to everyone. The light shines in the darkness, and the darkness can never extinguish it" (John 1:4–5). Jesus the Light of the world illuminates the darkness of the world.

John is clear. He writes that Mary went to the tomb "while it was still dark," but we know from Mark that the sun had already risen, and that Mary wouldn't go there anyway until the sunrise ended the Jewish Sabbath. The Law would not allow it. What's John teaching us here? I think it's simple. Mary's cave of hopelessness had plunged her into darkness. She thought that the light of the world had been taken away from her, which left her with no understanding of what was going on. It's hard to see things in the dark. It's hard to find your way forward in the dark. In her cave of hopelessness, Mary has lost sight of Jesus. She cried out: "They've taken the Lord's body, and we don't know where he is!"

The cave of hopelessness is where we cry out: "God, where are you? It wasn't supposed to be like this." For centuries, Christ-followers have called this "the dark night of the soul." Cheryl and I spent more than fifteen years in this cave as we sojourned with our son Nathan and his addiction. I remember more than once praying, "God, you've used our church and ministry to help thousands of people get clean and sober, but our precious son Nathan at the end of our hallway is dying. 'What's up God? Why God?'" It was place of no understanding.

It's really important for us to notice how Mary responds in the midst of no understanding. This is a good impulse for a contemporary Christ follower too. First, she returns to the other disciples. Peter and another disciple then run ahead of her back to the garden tomb. Finally, Mary follows the disciples to the place where Jesus should be. She goes where she thinks that she'll find him. She could have given up, gone home, put on her jammies, and binge-watched Netflix! But no, she refuses to give up her search. She returns to the tomb, this time with Peter and John. John recounts:

> Mary was standing outside the tomb crying, and as she wept, she stooped and looked in. She saw two white-robed angels, one sitting at the head and the other at the foot of the place where the body of Jesus had been lying. "Dear woman, why are you crying?" the angels asked her. "Because they have taken away my Lord," she replied, "and I don't know where they have put him." (John 20:11-13 NLT)

Mary still doesn't understand and frankly she shouldn't. Again, don't let the fact that *you* know the end of this story cloud things. When Mary comes back to the tomb, she discovers two angels sitting there folding laundry, Jesus' grave clothes. "Why are you crying?" they ask. "I cannot find the dead body of Jesus. Someone must have taken it," Mary responds. In her hopelessness, Mary cannot see an option. She's hopeless.

Here Mary begins the second leg of her journey in the cave of hopelessness because it was for Mary, and it can be for us a cave of misunderstanding. It's utter soul confusion. In this space, we tend to grasp for straws to simply make sense of the pain. Mary's journey through her confusion is described in John's commentary this way:

> She turned to leave and saw someone standing there. It was Jesus, but she didn't recognize him. "Dear woman, why are you crying?" Jesus asked her. "Who are you looking for?" She thought he was the gardener. "Sir," she said, "if you have taken him away, tell me where you have put him, and I will go and get him." (John 20:14-15 NLT)

The first two words are, "She turned." Mary's experience in her cave of hopelessness isn't done. No, understanding doesn't have the last word. Because as she turns away, she runs smack into Jesus standing right in front of her. But she didn't recognize him. What a powerful statement! The darkness of the cave of hopelessness can blind us to Jesus' presence, even though he might be right in front of us. It becomes a cave of confusing misunderstanding. We've all been there struggling to make sense in the darkness.

God is starting to open Mary's eyes to the limitless possibilities of redemption and resurrection, but she's not quite there yet. This is movement. I love the recovery phrase "Progress, not perfection"— this movement from no understanding to misunderstanding is progress for the hopeless Mary of Magdala.

I think it's a beautiful little detail that John gave us. *She thought he was the gardener.* Could John be taking us all the way back to the beginning, to Genesis 2, to a beautiful garden, where life is birthed and created where hope springs eternal? Sin has no place and death has no power in the garden because the Gardener is on duty. Maybe John added this detail reflecting back to the words of Jesus when Jesus taught his disciples in the Upper Room about "abiding," and he spoke "I am the true grapevine, and my Father is the gardener" (John 15:1 NLT).

Often in the cave of hopelessness, the tears of loss and the grief blind us to the presence of Jesus. The prisms of salty liquid in the corners of our eyes sting and blur our vision. We cannot see Jesus through the sorrow. Maybe the worst night of the decade and a half journey with Nathan was the evening we had to kick him out of our home. Our breaking point was that he had become so desperate in his addiction that he moved from stealing from Cheryl and me to my parents, who were living with us. With only a backpack and a cell phone, we sent him out into the darkness on foot to an unknown future. Where was God in all of this? Almost a decade later after Nathan was gratefully clean and sober he called me one day following a counseling appointment with his therapist. "Hey Dad," Nathan said. "Today we were taking about gratitude in my session and I wanted to tell you thank you for kicking me out of the house all those years ago. I realized today that that was the beginning of me finding my bottom." We could not see then, but God was there. It was a cave of hopeless misunderstanding.

So finally, our cave of hopelessness can be transformed from a hiding place to a holy place. Because for Mary and for us if we keep walking (and yes often it is a slow walk), the cave of hopelessness can be the cave of new understanding. The details of verse 16 are profound. "Mary!" Jesus said. She turned to him and cried out, "Rabboni!" (Hebrew for "Teacher") (John 20:16). She recognizes Jesus. As the sun rises over the City of David scattering the darkness, the Son of God stands before her in all his resurrection glory. The living Jesus dispels the hopelessness with his presence and brings with him new possibility.

And of all the things Jesus can say to her in this moment of hopeful recognition, he chooses one word: her name. Jesus calls her by name. There's an older worship song that I love titled "He Knows My Name" written by Tommy Walker. It's a song about an orphan boy whom Tommy met in an orphanage in the Philippines named Jerry.[43] Their first meeting they introduced themselves to one another and Jerry, the orphan, said, "We are friends, right?"" "That's right, Jerry, we're friends," responded Tommy. A little later, Jerry ran up to Tommy and said, "Hey, what's my name?" Tommy said "Jerry! I know your name. You're Jerry!" "We're friends, right?" "Yes, Jerry, we're friends." It hit Tommy that Jerry was an orphan who had a deep desire to be known. And it's not just the Jerry's of this world. It's all of us. That first Easter morning, Mary met the God who knows her name. The truth is that the God we love and serve knows each of our names. He even knows our nicknames!

And it was upon hearing her name through the voice of Jesus (remember her vision is still blurred) that misunderstanding becomes new understanding. She cries out "Teacher!" My dear friend and colleague at Grace Church, Pastor Arlene Jackson, has been and continues to be a companion with me as Cheryl and I navigate our relationship with Nathan. Again, when Nathan was at his worse and I was ready to throw up my arms in defeat, she wisely counseled me with these words. "Where there is life, there is hope." In the cave of hopelessness, we do not know when the Gardener will call us by name. In the chaos, we have to remember that where there is life, there is hope. Because with Jesus, there are always options.

---

43.   http://worship-with-us.org/wp-content/uploads/2012/11/A-Worship-Minute-May-18th-2014.pdf.

Chapter Seven: With Jesus in the Cave of Resurrection

Resurrection means the worst thing is never the last thing.
—*Fredrick Buechner, The Final Beast*

In the summer of 1988 after graduating from Asbury Theological Seminary, my parents gave me a family trip to Puerto Rico, the island of my birth. It had been more than a decade since I had visited. One of the sights to which I took my young family was the Parque del las Cavernas del Rio Camuy or the River Camuy Cave Park. This cave is the third largest underground cave system in the world and the Camuy River runs through it. The caverns are part of a large network of natural limestone caves and underground waterways carved out by the river. It's really a bunch of caves in one big cave.

For the past six chapters, we have been looking at six biblical stories about men and women who spent time in literal caves. These cave experiences were "defining moments" for these men and women of faith. I have suggested that just like these ancient characters, we too get ushered into our own contemporary caves for our own personal "defining moments."

Each of the caves we have looked at in this book is really just like the River Camuy Cave system. Each is just a smaller cave within one big cave system called "the cave of life."

- In chapter 1, we went with Samson to the cave of anger. Samson needed a lot of therapy. He killed thirty people at a party that was thrown in honor of his engagement. Then a few days later, he killed one thousand people with the jawbone of a donkey. This boy had anger issues! We've been there.

- In chapter 2, we visited the cave of fear with David. On the run from a jealous and murderous King Saul, David and a band of hooligans hid deep in the cave of fear paralyzed by their dangerous circumstances. We've been there.

- In chapter 3, Elijah took us to the cave of depression. After an unbelievable battle with the prophets of Baal on Mount Carmel, literally and emotionally Elijah slipped into a dark cave of depression. He could not see his way out. It was just too dark. We've been there.

- Jesus helped us understand the cave of temptation in chapter 4. Satan tempted Jesus with the same stuff we get tempted with. His devilish tempter wanted Jesus to lose his identity as the beloved of the Father. We've been there.

- Chapter 5 brought us to the cave of grief. Mary and Martha agonized over the death of their brother. Grief like a tsunami drowned them in their sadness. Their brother was dead. They were lost in grief. We've been there.

- And then, in chapter 6 we journeyed to the cave of hopelessness with Mary Magdalene. Her future was blown apart with Jesus' death. It was the ultimate Now what? moment. She had put all her chips in with Jesus. He was her future. She had no options, no hope. We've been there.

Each of these caves make up the journey of our lives. The question is not an "If" question, but really a "When" question.

And let's be honest. The journey into these caves is not a "one and done" experience. Anger and grief ebb and flow in our lives. Depression and temptation come and go. Grief and hopelessness come knocking at our door again and again. One of my struggles as an author has been that I have not wanted to dumb down the complexities of these cave-time experiences while at the same time hope to offer a path of redemption and healing as we journey through them. Even as I write these words, the phone rang and it was an old dear friend with whom I served on staff years ago. His ministry is going splendidly but his family is experiencing excruciating recovery from agonizing trauma. This is the ugly possibility and beautiful potential that is life.

Each of these biblical characters we have considered experienced the reality that life is a contact sport leaving us bruised. Life is "iffy." It's got a big "I-F" in the middle of it. L-<u>IF</u>-E! Like the smaller caves in River Camuy Cave Park, each empties out into a larger cave system that we call "life," which brings with it the potential of pain and sorrow.

Jesus told us it would be this way. Remember that Jesus himself said in John 16:33b: "Here on earth you will have many trials and sorrows." We have all found this verse to be true while visiting these caves. Jesus did not promise that life would be without its hardships. As a matter of fact, the Bible teaches that God uses these journeys into our own personal caves, and they can be seasons for the shaping of our character and the building of our faith. That's why I have repeatedly said that a cave can either be a hiding place or a holy place, a place of concealing or a place of healing.

Your season in your own unique cave is a place of choice. Will you allow this season, of anger or fear or whatever cave you're in, destroy you or develop you? Will you hide from God or will you seek God? You and I get to choose. Those biblical characters who sought

God in their caves were transformed by their cave experience. Their character was built and their faith was increased!

Followers of Jesus have to remember that Jesus told his disciples just hours before his crucifixion all that he and they would endure. Look again at the entirety of what Jesus said in John 16:33: "I have told you all this so that you may have peace in me. Here on earth you will have many trials and sorrows. But take heart, because I have overcome the world." Yes, we will have troubles. Yes, we will do cave time, but we can rest assured that no matter what the world throws our way, we are connected to the One who has overcome the world! Notice it says, "So that *in me* you may have peace." Followers of Jesus are given the promise of supernatural peace. You see, there is one more cave into which we can journey. It's our pilgrimage into the cave of resurrection with Jesus.

Into the Cave of Resurrection with Jesus

More than any of the caves we have visited, this cave is a cave of victory. This is the cave of overcoming. This is a cave of deliverance. You know the old, old story. The religious and political leaders conspired together to kill Jesus. For three days from Friday late afternoon to Sunday early morning, Jesus is dead. No breath. No pulse. No blood flow. Nothing!

Then on early Sunday morning, Matthew's biography tells us Mary Magdalene and another Mary made their way to the tomb, a cave where Jesus had been buried just three days earlier. An earthquake and an angel rolled away the stone from the cave. It was not to let Jesus out, but to let them (and us) see in. Mary looks in and sees an angel. Matthew 28:5-6 tells us what the angel said. Then the angel spoke to the women. "Don't be afraid!" he said. "I know you are looking for Jesus, who was crucified. He isn't here! He is risen from the dead, just as he said would happen. Come, see where his body was lying." Jesus' cave of death was empty. What they expected to see was not there. "He is not here! He has risen!" It's the cave of resurrection.

Things are not always as they appear to be. The God we love and serve is masterful at transformation, and nothing screams this louder than Jesus' resurrection from the dead. Death was what was expected. The Marys came expecting a dead body for them to tend to with burial spices, but instead they found an empty tomb. Fredrick Buechner the great writer on this spiritual life wrote:

> Resurrection means the worst thing is never the last thing. The worst thing is the next to the last thing. The last thing is the best. It's the power from on high that comes down into the world, that wells up from the rock-bottom worst of the world like a hidden spring. Can you believe it? The last, best thing is the laughing deep in the hearts of the saints, sometimes our hearts even. Yes. You are terribly loved and forgiven. Yes. You are healed. All is well. [44]

"Resurrection means that the worst thing is never the last thing." The worst thing for the Marys, the disciples, and the band of Jesus followers happened on Good Friday. Jesus was dead. Hands that touched to heal, feet that walked to the people nobody else wanted or saw, lips that spoke words of hope, all were lifeless on Friday. But as Tony Campolo so masterfully says, "It's a Friday, but Sunday's a comin'!" Surprise! The worst thing is never the last thing in God's economy!

In the South American country of Chile, there is a barren land called the Atacama Desert. It is a huge desert stretching 990 miles and is commonly known as the driest spot on our planet. It gets less than 6/10ths of an inch of rain a year. There are even spots in this huge desert that have never received rain, not ever. Because it is so dry and arid, NASA uses the Atacama Desert to test landing rovers, as the environment is so much like Mars. But there is also another

---

44. Buechner, *The Final Beast* (HarperCollins, 1982), 175.

amazing and interesting dynamic in this desert wasteland. Just beneath the surface of the desert are the seeds for over two hundred different kinds of flowers. Imagine that.

Every once in a while, the Atacama Desert gets a year's worth of rain in a day. It happened in 2015, and when it does, something amazing and mysterious happens. This desert graveyard turns into a "super bloom." A wasteland turns into a garden. We serve a God who turns graves into gardens. If you feel like your life is a desert, I want to remind you that there is a "super bloom" waiting to explode in you. In God's Kingdom, the last thing does not have the final word.

Easter Sunday, Resurrection Day, is all about this kind of "superbloom" transformation. It's about the worst thing not being the last thing. It's about surprises. It's about experiencing what is not expected. And God wants to do his transformational work in you. The question really is: How can Jesus transform me in the cave of resurrection? What can happen to me as I peer into the cave of resurrection?

Wounds into Scars

Now I could spend countless pages answering these questions, but I want to focus on one aspect of the transformation Jesus can do for us in the cave of resurrection. Here's my best answer to the question, How can Jesus transform me in the cave of resurrection? It's pretty simple. Jesus transforms my wounds into his scars. Say that out loud right now. "Jesus transforms my wounds into his scars." Stop and reflect on this statement.

Go with me back a few days before Easter Sunday. After Jesus' arrest and kangaroo court of the religious and political leaders of Jerusalem, Jesus is beaten almost to death. Then he carries the cross down the road we now call the Via Delarosa. Once on the outskirts of Jerusalem, on a garbage heap called Golgotha, the Place of Skull, Jesus is nailed to the cross. Matthew 27:35 gives us this matter-of-fact commentary: "After they had nailed him to the cross, the soldiers gambled for his clothes by throwing dice."

Historians tell us that the Roman crucifixion was extremely painful. Typically, spikes were driven between the bones of the lower arm just above the wrist. There isn't always agreement as to how the spikes were nailed to the feet. Some had them nailed to the side of the cross while others think his feet were nailed to a footrest. Regardless, Jesus lingered for hours before dying somewhere around 3:00 p.m. on that awful Friday. These spikes left wounds on Jesus' body.

John's biography of Jesus is the one of the four Gospels that gives us this little detail about the wound in Jesus' side. Asphyxiation was the cause of death for Roman crucifixion. The crucified would stand on the spike to breath in and relax to breath out but it was extremely painful to do so. When exhaustion took over, they would simple smother and die. To hurry along the deaths of the three men crucified that day, the Romans broke the legs of the two who hung with Jesus. But by the time they got to Jesus, he was already dead. To make sure he was dead, John19:34 gives us this detail of what they did "One of the soldiers . . . pierced his side with a spear, and immediately blood and water flowed out." The lack of any physical reaction by Jesus to a sharp spear in his side assured the Romans that Jesus was indeed dead. This spear left a wound on Jesus too.

So stay with me. Three days later, Jesus is resurrected. On that day, the two Marys tell the other disciples that Jesus is alive. Later that first Easter Sunday evening, Jesus mysteriously appears to the fearful disciples locked away in a home. He says to them, "Peace be with you," and then John 20:20 (NIV) gives us this detail: "As he spoke, he showed them the wounds in his hands and his side. They were filled with joy when they saw the Lord!" Jesus showed them his "scars." Notice I did not say his "wounds." I said scars. There is a huge difference.

I have been thinking about this difference a lot. Wounds have to be treated. Sometimes people have to go to "wound care centers" to get still-sensitive, unhealed wounds treated. Wounds need care and attention. Scars do not. Scars are healed wounds. Scars tell stories.

I have four scars on my body. When I was about two, an older girl swung a teeter-totter at me and hit me just below my eye. It left me with a bunch of stitches and a sad story of being beaten up by a girl. When I was a sophomore in high school, I took a hit to the inside of my right knee. In the days before orthoscopic surgery, my knee surgery meant hours of surgery, followed by days of hospitalization, followed by months of rehab. I have a scar about six inches long on my right knee that tells a story of what someone else did to hurt me. About two years later, against my father's rules, I was playing sandlot football and caught a pass, only to land in a pile of glass. I have stitches on my right arm that tell a story of my disobedience to my father. Finally, in December of 2021, after years of nursing my left knee, my orthopedic surgeon and I determined it was time for a total knee replacement. A long eight-inch scar is the result. Each of my scars tells a different story. They are testimonies of what others did to me or I did to myself that left an injury. A scar is a wound that has healed. Here's the deal. Jesus' crucifixion wounds became his resurrection scars. His wounds told the story of his anguish, suffering, and death, but his scars told the story of his glorious resurrection!

Let me ask you, in the contact sport that is your life, in the "iffy-ness" that is your life, do you have wounds or scars? Here's how you know the difference. Are you still lost in your cave of anger, fear, depression, temptation, grief, or hopelessness? It doesn't matter if you got yourself in there or if somebody else put you there. It's still a wound. As a pastor, one of the things that breaks my heart is seeing so many followers of Jesus living with open wounds. Sadly, they never leave their caves and live with the pain that has either been self-inflicted or inflicted upon them by others. But if they'd let Jesus' resurrection power draw them out of their cave, then they'd have a story to tell and they'd have a scar to prove it.

One of the gifts of staying at the same church for decades is walking with people throughout the seasons of their lives. I have had the privilege of marrying women and men whom I baptized as babies. I've also had the painful privilege of walking with men and women who for whatever reason refused to step into the cave of resurrection and have Jesus transform their wounds into scars. I think of an old friend, now dead. I do not think there was a time that I was with my friend that he wasn't drunk. At the same time, our recovery ministry was exploding and was helping hundreds of people be set free from their addictions, afflictions, and compulsive behaviors. I'd put my arm around my friend and say, "Your miracle is fifty feet away. Just walk in that room over there and you'll find a community of drunks to help you get well." Sadly, my dear friend died a drunk. He died with unhealed wounds.

Saul, one of the greatest followers of Jesus, had many wounds. He had spent lots of days in caves of anger, hatred, and bigotry, killing some of the first followers of Jesus. Then Saul met Jesus. His name was changed to Paul and his wounds became his scars. In Galatians 6:17 we find these powerful words that he wrote: "From now on, don't let anyone trouble me with these things. For I bear on my body the scars that show I belong to Jesus." Paul had scars that became his testimony that showed he belonged to Jesus. The cave of resurrection did that for Paul and it can do it for you.

As only God could orchestrate, during Holy Week 2016, my family got an early Easter gift on Monday afternoon about 1:45. It happened at the Lee County Courthouse in Courtroom 5G with the honorable Judge Hayes presiding. Our precious son Nathan who has suffered untold misery because of his addiction to drugs graduated from Drug Court. After more than a decade of wandering in and out of caves of anger, fear, depression, temptation, grief, and hopelessness, on Monday, Nathan emerged from the cave of resurrection, clean and sober.

God is in the business of turning our wounds into scars, and Jesus wants to do that for you. The cave of resurrection declares that your wounds do not have to win. God can transform your wounds into His scars. He is the One who rose victorious over sin, death, hell, and the grave, and he did all of this for you!

In Mark's account of this first Easter, he shares that the women also entered the tomb to find Jesus but he is not there. An angel is. Mark reveals that their assignment to go tell the others had specific instructions for one disciple in particular. Look at Mark 16:5-7:

> When they entered the tomb, they saw a young man clothed in a white robe sitting on the right side. The women were shocked, but the angel said, "Don't be alarmed. You are looking for Jesus of Nazareth, who was crucified. He isn't here! He is risen from the dead! Look, this is where they laid his body. Now go and tell his disciples, including Peter, that Jesus is going ahead of you to Galilee. You will see him there, just as he told you before he died." (NLT)

The assignment is for them to tell all the disciples, but one in particular. Which one? Peter. Why? Well, I think it's because he especially is on Jesus' mind. Peter was brash, confident, and reckless in his love and devotion for Jesus. But when the pressure was on, when it was crunch time, Peter blew it. He denies knowing Jesus. Jesus had warned him about this. But still, Peter folded, leaving not only his Savior but his friend Jesus alone. Peter is devastated. When a rooster crows Peter knows that Jesus also knows. The tears soon follow like a salty spring. But the angel delivers this news that we can easily miss. "Tell the disciples . . . AND Peter." Jesus wanted to turn Peter's wounds into scars. They would become his testimony.

Go with me back to John 11 and the story of the death of Jesus' dear friend Lazarus, brother to Mary and Martha. Remember that

Jesus was "good and mad" at what death did to those he loved. John records that Jesus spoke three words to death. "Then Jesus shouted, "Lazarus, come out!" (John 11:43). I wonder if Jesus might be speaking these words with your name instead of Lazarus'. "(Insert your name) come out!"

There is a painting that Vincent Van Gogh painted in 1890 while in residence at Saint-Paul Asylum in Saint-Rémy, France, called "The Raising of Lazarus." It was based on a Rembrandt etching that Van Gogh's brother had sent him. But while Rembrandt's etchings and paintings of Lazarus focused on Jesus, Van Gogh left Jesus out of the picture and focused on Lazarus and the two sisters, Mary and Martha. Some think Lazarus' face is a self-portrait, pointing to the red beard resembling Van Gogh's own. If true, then Van Gogh powerfully and profoundly painted himself as the one who needed resurrection.

Where do you need a resurrection in your life? Where are you like Lazarus? In what way are you dead today? Jesus is here and the same God who spoke the world into existence and spoke life into Lazarus' dead body wants to speak resurrection into you. Is it your relationship with God that needs new life? Are you spiritually dead? Let today be your Easter. It is a great day for fresh starts and new beginnings. Remember that Lazarus didn't do a thing to earn his resurrection. It was a gift of grace. Today, Jesus is saying to you "Come out!"

I can remember the very first time that I experienced Jesus care for and heal my wounds. It was one of my "Jorge, come out" moments. It happened to me on Easter 1983. That was the morning our first son, Daniel Aaron Acevedo, was born. Before I began following Jesus in 1978, I was lost in a world of drinking, drugging, and sexual promiscuity. By April 1983, I had been a Christ-follower for five years, and I had been called by God into fulltime ministry. I was a junior at Asbury College working on a degree in Bible. Yet because of all of the hurt and damage I had inflected on women, I lived with deep seated guilt, shame, and condemnation.

My dirty little "soul secret," my soul wound, was that I thought I did not deserve a child because of all my sexual sins. Cheryl went into labor on Saturday, April 2, and gave birth at 3:45 a.m. on Sunday, April 3, 1983, . . . Easter Sunday morning. As I held Daniel for the first time in my arms, I looked out the window and saw people across the parking lot at Centenary United Methodist Church getting ready for their Easter Sunrise service. It was then that I heard a whisper from the Holy Spirit. "Jorge, today is the day that the world celebrates when I gave my Son for the forgiveness of their sins. But today is also the day that I gave you your son so that you might know my forgiveness." Easter 1983, the Good News of Jesus' resurrection was told to his disciples . . . and Jorge. That morning, Jesus healed my wounds and I've never been the same. I now have a scar and testimony. And because God loves me so much, our second son, Nathan Kyle Acevedo, was born on Valentine's Day . . . on a Sunday! On the day the world celebrates love, God gave me a second gift of love in case my Easter miracle ever waned. Jesus transformed my cave of self-condemnation into a cave of resurrection.

For two summers in a row, Cheryl and I took high school students backpacking in the mountains of Montana back in the early 90s. The first year we went, our guide was like a mixture between James Bond and Indiana Jones. One afternoon on an all-day hike, we found ourselves in freezing rain and sleet on a granite mountaintop at 11,000 feet above sea level and we were never afraid. Why? We had an experienced guide! The next summer, our James Bond/Indiana Jones guide was unavailable and he sent us his, shall I say, "less than competent" son. We were about four hours into a sixteen-hour hike when we heard the words you never want to hear your guide say. "Uh oh! We're lost!" This was bad . . . really bad! What made the difference in the two experiences? It was the skill and trustworthiness of the guide.

Jesus is a trustworthy guide for your life, for now and for eternity. When you are lost in the caves of life, he will find you. When you are afraid, he will comfort you. When you need guidance, he will guide you. And when life this side of the grave is over, he can be trusted to lead us through the sorrows of this life and to eternity with God. From the cradle to the grave from our first breath to our last, Jesus can be our reliable Leader. That's why in John 14:6a, Jesus says of himself: *"I am the way and the truth and the life."* Jesus is a good guide and if you don't know what to do, let Jesus guide you through the caves of life!

On Good Friday 2018, we gathered together in the sanctuary of Grace Church and celebrated the life of one of God's amazing Christ-followers, my brother in Christ Miguel Fernandez. I have known Miguel, his wife, Denise, and their three beautiful daughters over the course of nearly three decades that I have served at Grace Church. When I came to Grace Church, we got along marvelously, he as a Cuban and me as a Puerto Rican. I watched over the years as God deepened the faith of this "cradle" Methodist brother. I observed as he and Denise championed our ministry with our sister church in Cuba. He also served our church and community as a missionary. Maybe it was because his family had been forced out of Cuba by Fidel Castro that Miguel treasured his life, his family, this church, and this community.

In 2015, Miguel was diagnosed with cancer and told he might only live a few months. With even greater vigor, he fought the disease while double downing on making memories, especially with his family. I never once in the three years heard Miguel ask, "Why me?" Instead he asked, "Why not me?" and he kept serving God as an attorney, family man, church, and community leader. He washed feet at our Shoes of Hope outreach, served on hospitality teams, joined a men's small group, and led in community events. He stayed on mission with Jesus until the very end.

Cheryl and I went to Lee Memorial Hospital to see Miguel on the Sunday night before he died the following Wednesday. I was flying to Los Angeles for a denominational meeting the next morning. When I entered his room, he was wearing an oxygen mask that forced air into his lungs. Miguel saw me and at once began to sing the doxology in Spanish through his mask! Even as he was facing death, he was praising God. This is the heart of a fearless Christ follower. As the book of Acts said of David (Acts 13:36), Miguel served the purposes of God in his generation and then he died. And he followed Jesus his guide into and through the cave of resurrection. For Miguel, death did not have the final word. Life did. Miguel never tasted death. He passed from temporal life here to life eternal as Jesus ushered him to eternity. This is the promise we hold onto as we journey through life's caves.

Conclusion

When I was a student at Asbury Theological Seminary, a dear friend, Hule, and fellow youth pastor took me on my first rock climbing adventure. We made the seventy-mile trip from Wilmore, Kentucky, to the Red River Gorge, where Hule began teaching me the art and science of rock climbing. He taught me how to put on a harness and loop the ropes safety and securely through a figure 8 belay device. All of this helped me both climb up and rappel down rugged rock faces at the Gorge.

Then Hule taught me the language of rock climbing. One very important word in rock climbing that I learned is *belay*. To belay someone means that the person on the ground takes the slack out of the rope so that if the climber falls he or she does not hit the ground. The belayer wears a harness with a belay device to assist in this important lifesaving task. There are a series of commands that we would use to assure that everyone involved had a safe journey up and down the rock face. So, for example, when I was ready to begin my climb, I'd shout, "On belay?" that was in essence asking my partner, "Hey, are you ready to belay me? Have you got me as I make my ascent up the rock?" If my belayer was ready, he or she would shout back loudly and clearly, "Belay on!" which in essence means, "I've got you. The slack is out of the rope. Climb on."

At some point in life, all of us will have to climb deep into the crevasses of life called caves. These are those dangerous climbs when by personal choice or by somebody else's choosing, we enter into a potentially life-threatening gorge. These caves have different names. Sometimes we call them *death* or *divorce*. Sometimes they are called *discouragement* or *depression*. The names change but the hazard is the same.

But we are not alone. God meets us in these dark, perilous places. He wants to be our belayer. Look at how the prophet Isaiah describes the context of God's care in these dangerous caves:

> But now, O Jacob, listen to the LORD who created you. O Israel, the one who formed you says, "Do not be afraid, for I have ransomed you. I have called you by name; you are mine. When you go through deep waters, I will be with you. When you go through rivers of difficulty, you will not drown. When you walk through the fire of oppression, you will not be burned up; the flames will not consume you. For I am the LORD, your God, the Holy One of Israel, your Savior." (Isaiah 43:1-3a NLT)

Whether the waters are deep or the fire is hot, the God who made you and me is with us. We will not drown or be consumed. This is God's promise and it can be trusted. So, we say to God, "On belay?" and God says, "Belay on!"

9 781953 495518